LEARNING

The Official FA Guide to
Psychology for Football

LEARNING

The Official FA Guide to
Psychology for Football

Dr Andy Cale and Roberto Forzoni

Contributors
Paul Dent
Allison Dyer
Jim Lowther

Hodder Arnold

A MEMBER OF THE HODDER HEADLINE GROUP

For order enquiries: please contact Bookpoint Ltd, 130 Milton Park, Abingdon, Oxon
OX14 4SB. Telephone: +44 (0) 1235 827720. Fax: +44 (0) 1235 400454. Lines are open
from 09.00–17.00, Monday to Saturday with a 24-hour message-answering service.
Details about our titles and how to order are available at www.hoddereducation.com

British Library Cataloguing in Publication Data:
a catalogue record for this title is available from the British Library.

ISBN 9 780340 816011

First Published 2004
Impression number   10 9 8 7 6
Year   2007

Managing Editor: Jonathan Wilson, FA Learning

Typeset by Servis Filmsetting Ltd, Manchester.
Printed in Great Britain for Hodder Arnold, a division of Hodder Headline, An Hachette
Livre UK Company, 338 Euston Road, London NW1 3BH by Cox & Wyman, Reading,
Berkshire.

The publisher has used its best endeavours to ensure that the URLs for external websites
referred to in this book are correct and active at the time of going to press. However, the
publisher and the author have no responsibility for the websites and can make no
guarantee that a site will remain live or that the content will remain relevant, decent or
appropriate.

Hodder Headline's policy is to use papers that are natural, renewable and recyclable
products and made from wood grown in sustainable forests. The logging and
manufacturing processes are expected to conform to the environmental regulations of the
country of origin.

Contents

LEARNING

Philosophy of the guides

The aim of these **Official FA Guides** is to reach the millions of people who participate in football or who are involved in the game in other ways – at any level.

Each book aims to increase your awareness and understanding of association football and in this understanding to enhance, increase, improve and extend your involvement in the world's greatest game.

These books are designed to be interactive and encourage you to apply what you read and to help you to translate this knowledge into practical skills and ability. Specific features occur throughout this book to assist this process:

■   Tasks will appear in this form and will make you think about what you have just learned and how you will apply it in a practical way.

Best Practice   The Best Practice feature will give you an example of a good or ideal way of doing things – this could be on or off the pitch.

Quote | 'Quotes throughout will pass on useful knowledge or insight or encourage you to consider a certain aspect of your skills or responsibilities.'

Statistic

The statistics included will often surprise and will certainly increase your knowledge of the game.

Summary

- **The summaries at the end of each chapter will recap on its contents and help you to consolidate your knowledge and understanding.**

You can read this guide in any way you choose and prefer to do so – at home, on the pitch, in its entirety, or to dip in for particular advice. Whatever way you use it, we hope it increases your ability, your knowledge, your involvement, and most importantly your enjoyment and passion to **be a part of the game**.

Introduction

THIS CHAPTER WILL:
- Introduce you to sport psychology.
- Explain how sport psychology may help your players to develop.
- Describe the format and contents of this book.
- Suggest ways of getting the best out of this book.

A key reason for studying sport psychology in football is to improve your awareness of players as individuals, understand why children play football, explore what motivates them, learn how to improve their confidence, control and commitment and, most of all, how to ensure players continue to have fun during their football experience.

Sport psychology

So what is sport psychology and how can it help you in the training and development of your players? Basically, psychology is the study of the mind. Sport psychology is the scientific study of people and their behaviours in sport.

How sport psychology might help your players

The aim of using sport psychology is to employ sound principles and research to help player development by gaining an understanding of the following:

- Why players participate in the sport.
- What motivates players to try football and then maintain their involvement.
- How self-confidence can be built up in players.
- How to develop a team that performs better than the sum of its parts.

The main objective of this book is to introduce, in plain language, some of the many concepts of sport psychology. It will help you start to understand the effects of psychological factors on physical performance, for example:

- How anxiety may affect a player taking a penalty kick.
- How a lack of self-confidence may cause a player to drop out of the sport.
- How a coach's comments and use of rewards may influence the team's motivation.
- How imagery training may help a player score from a free kick.
- How parents and coaches can enrich the football experience of players.

How to use this book

The Official FA Guide to Psychology for Football has been put together to give you a basic and practical understanding of how you might introduce elements of sport psychology into your team. Each chapter will start with a list of learning outcomes, i.e. what you can learn by reading that chapter. Each chapter includes many tasks and examples of best practice, and each finishes with a summary, some self-tester questions and an action plan for you to put the ideas into practice.

The book is written so that it can be used as a tool that you can simply dip in and out of. If you are interested in imagery, for example, you can go straight to Chapter 8 – and away you go!

Summary

- **The introduction to sport psychology offers a basic description and explanation of some simple sport psychology techniques and strategies that can be used to help your children develop as people and as players. It can help to improve their rate of development in football. Major concepts such as motivation, confidence, goal-setting and team building are introduced.**

Self testers

1 What is sport psychology?

2 How might sport psychology help your players?

3 What is the best way to use this book?

Action plan

Set aside 30 minutes a day to read one chapter of this book   Then, with the help of the suggested tasks and action plans, decide how you might adapt your coaching by using some of the techniques in that chapter to create a more positive coaching environment.

Chapter 1

The player

> THIS CHAPTER WILL:
> - Demonstrate the importance of getting to know your players.
> - Explore reasons why young players play football.
> - Help you to get the best out of your players.
> - Explain the benefits of developing a player-centred approach to your coaching.
> - Explore psychological techniques which may help you to develop your players.

It is amazing how many coaches attempt to motivate their team, give the team confidence and create a winning team without really getting to know the most important part of the team – the individual player!

Get to know your players

Quote | 'How can I motivate my players?'
'How can I get the best from them?'
'Why are they not trying hard tonight?'

The quotes on the previous page demonstrate some elusive questions that many coaches or managers of junior football clubs often ask. By gaining a greater understanding and awareness of your players as individuals, you may put yourself in a position where the answers to these questions come more easily.

Tables 1 and 2 show sample sheets compiled to help you to get to know your players. Some of the questions appear irrelevant to the development of football players but remember, we are in the business of developing people first – players second! On reading through the various chapters of this book, you will soon come to realize that the more you know about your players, their fears, concerns, likes, dislikes and so on, the more able you will be to help them in their development.

■ Think of some other questions that you could add to a personal information sheet for your players.

The next time you take a session, ask yourself 'Do I really know my players? What makes them tick? Why are they here?'

Quote | 'Players care what you know when they know you care!'

You will notice that Table 2 contains a box where the player can fill out their personal football statement. The reason for this is to allow the player to explore and identify some of his or her strengths – a key aspect in confidence building for later on. Typical responses may include the following:

- 'I am a really quick and sharp winger who loves to dribble past a full-back and put in a good cross.'
- 'I am a mid-field player who loves a tackle and wants to get forward to score goals.'

Table 1 **Sample player information sheet 1**

Team United FC
Under 13
Personal information

Name:	DOB:	School year:	Best position:
Dad's name:	Mum's name:	Brother(s): (ages)	Sister(s): (ages)

Three ...	**1**	**2**	**3**
... things that make you *feel good* in a game			
... things that you *like to do* in training			
... television programmes you watch			
... books you've read			
... magazines you read			
... favourite films			
... favourite football players			
... favourite sports stars (any sport)			
... favourite foods			
... favourite drinks			
... favourite CDs			
... favourite football teams you like to watch			
... strengths of your game			
... areas you would like to improve in your game			
... things you'd like to achieve this year			

Table 2 **Sample player information sheet 2**

Team United FC
Under 13
Personal information

	1	2	3
My favourite professional player			
... three reasons why			
My favourite player in my current side			
... three reasons why			
My strengths in football (in training)			
My strengths in football (match specific – if different)			
Pictures/objects/animals/ symbols that reflect my strengths			
My strengths in life (general)			
My personal football statement: 'I am ...			
State how discipline at school or at home can help your football performance:			
What use is a good education to a professional football player?			

These statements are written in the present tense (I am) and they contain positives (thoughts and/or behaviours). They should also be written in the player's own language, not the coach's. The reference to school and education in Table 2 allows the player to explore issues with learning, and to reflect on the importance of having as good an education as possible, not neglecting schooling simply because they are playing football.

Making the time to find out this additional information will give you a further perspective on your players, and help to build a rapport that can enhance development on the training field and beyond.

Why do people play football?

If you asked a young footballer why they play the game, they would probably offer one of the following reasons:

- I have a lot of fun playing.
- I enjoy myself.

- I want to be with my friends.
- I enjoy competing.
- I enjoy showing my skills.
- I want to improve my skills.
- I want to be part of a team.
- I get a sense of achievement.
- I enjoy copying my favourite player!
- I want to be a professional football player.
- It's fun!

Statistic

In England over 250,000 children play Mini Soccer.

Many different reasons will surface, but the key reason appears to be simply the satisfaction and enjoyment of playing – the fun part. Sometimes this occurs both in training and matches; other times, the satisfaction of training exceeds the pleasure of match play, dependent upon the type of child and, more importantly, the type of environment you, the coach, create.

■ Make a list of your players and identify what you think is their main reason for participation. After doing this, go and ask them what their reasons are for participation. How close were you in your predictions? Do you need to change your expectations/goals for individual players or for the team as a whole?

Best Practice Remember your players are playing football to have fun!
Keep it fun!

Develop a player-centred approach

A basic principle of using sport psychology with players is firstly to be aware of your responsibility as a coach or manager in ensuring that the player is the key to everything. The player should be the focal point of your attention. Develop an attitude that it is your responsibility to the young player, as an adult coach, to continue to improve your own skills and knowledge to enable you to better understand and support your players. Be there for the player's benefit.

Best Practice Develop a player-centred philosophy. Constantly try to improve your own knowledge for the players' benefit.

Player first, winning second

If fun and enjoyment are key reasons for young players participating in sport, then the more the coach can do to promote a positive experience the better! One major cause for concern and anxiety in players is a constant reference to the importance of winning; not only in competitive matches, but also in training. If young players look upon themselves as failures when losing, they may quickly develop poor motivation to continue; they may worry more and not persist at difficult tasks. In essence, their development will be severely impaired. Sven-Göran Eriksson refers to this as a 'fear of failure'. (*Sven-Göran Eriksson on Football*, 2001, Carlton Books) It stops players from being creative, taking chances in the game, and gaining satisfaction from the process of competing rather than simply from the outcome (i.e. the result). Instead of emphasizing winning, coaches should encourage self-improvements. If players are afraid to make mistakes, their learning and development may be slowed down. Players are much more likely to enjoy playing and develop at a faster rate if they are encouraged to concentrate on personal improvement at the expense of simply winning. This does not imply that players are discouraged from striving to win football matches; it simply means changing the focus for the benefit of player development.

Best Practice If to win merely means to beat, then the player will invariably experience frustration and disappointment which can increase the chances of them dropping out from the sport. Develop an attitude of personal improvement over and above winning.

▨ Start emphasizing personal and team improvement rather than winning in all your training sessions and matches.

Keep communication lines open

Children like to know they can talk to their coach. When the child perceives the coach as always being too busy to talk – 'Not having time for me' or even, 'Why would he want to hear what I have to say?' – great opportunities to get to know your players may pass. Gerard Houllier, Liverpool's manager, often refers to the fact that he makes sure he spends time every day just mixing with players and chatting; showing he cares about them. They in turn are more likely to discuss matters with him. These may simply be small issues, but occasionally they could be important issues for the players that the coach may never have known had he not given the player time.

Some players may perform below their usual standards for reasons totally unbeknown to the coach. There may be issues at home, at school, or with friends or teammates. Having an 'open door' policy, or simply speaking to each player about an issue outside football at least once every session may lead to big rewards in terms of player–coach trust and player development.

Good coaches also allow players to have a say in their development. Feedback is a two-way concept! This does not always come easy to inexperienced coaches, and it does not mean that players are in charge of what goes on. In a structured programme, there should be some flexibility with regards to allowing players some say in how they train.

For quality communication to occur between two people, one person needs to talk and the other person is required to listen. In the majority of cases, the harder skill is that of listening. See Chapter 6 for a more detailed discussion of communication.

Best Practice Keep the 'communication' door nicely open for your players. Do not ignore players who need help. It is up to you to either give support or suggest someone who can help the player. Don't be afraid to let players contribute to their football development. Be an unbelievably good listener so that you really hear what your player says.

■ Organize a short amount of time each month at the beginning of one of your sessions to ask players their opinions in relation to: the team, the players, or your coaching style!

A player diary

A useful tool for managers and coaches is an individual player diary. Many coaches have no idea about players' commitments and how they really feel throughout the week. How much other physical training does your player take part in? A school cross-country run, school athletics,

gym and so forth can all take their toll and affect a player's motivation, confidence and commitment to your football programme. Why does a player look like he or she is not interested in that practice that took you ages to prepare? The answer may be much easier to determine if you know a little more about your players' lifestyles.

Best Practice Use a weekly player diary to monitor a player's physical activities throughout the week. A diary can be a great source of player motivation. Diaries can provide players with a responsibility that can help develop ownership and confidence.

A sample diary is shown in Table 3 and was developed primarily for 10–14-year-old players so that they could list and monitor their physical activities, not only their football commitments but also their other weekly commitments. With this diary, the coach can better understand and react to the individual player's needs. Furthermore, the diary has an added section for players to record details about their goals and objectives for the week.

Diaries can be customized to reflect your own requirements and any specific aims that you may have as a coach. Setting weekly goals can be particularly beneficial (see Chapter 7 on goal-setting).

▨　Develop a player diary for your players to complete on a weekly basis. Personalize the diary to include aspects of importance for your team.

Quote | 'The mind is like a parachute. It works better when it is open.'

Table 3 **Sample player weekly diary**

My weekly diary   **Week commencing Monday ....**

Football activity			Other physical activities		
Monday		Hours			Hours
Club			School		
School			After-school		
Match			Evening		
Fitness			Other		
Tuesday		Hours			Hours
Club			School		
School			After-school		
Match			Evening		
Fitness			Other		
Wednesday		Hours			Hours
Club			School		
School			After-school		
Match			Evening		
Fitness			Other		
Thursday		Hours			Hours
Club			School		
School			After-school		
Match			Evening		
Fitness			Other		

Friday		Hours			Hours
Club			School		
School			After-school		
Match			Evening		
Fitness			Other		

Saturday		Hours			Hours
Club			School		
School			After-school		
Match			Evening		
Fitness			Other		

Sunday		Hours			Hours
Club			School		
School			After-school		
Match			Evening		
Fitness			Other		

Main weekly targets and objectives

This week I am working on	
I need to improve this because	
And when I achieve this it would mean	

I use self-talk by continually telling myself (see Chapter 3)	
I use imagery by seeing myself (see Chapter 8)	
I focused by	
I am using my routines to	

Table 4 shows a sample completed diary page.

Table 4 **Sample completed diary sheet**

My weekly diary **Week commencing Monday** ....

Football activity			Other physical activities		

Monday

Football activity		Hours	Other physical activities		Hours
Club	Club Training night		School	Athletics	
School			After-school		1
Match	Worked on keep-ups & dribbling		Evening		
Fitness			Other		

Tuesday

Football activity		Hours	Other physical activities		Hours
Club			School		
School			After-school		
Match			Evening		
Fitness			Other		

Wednesday

Football activity		Hours	Other physical activities		Hours
Club	Club Training	2	School		
School			After-school		
Match	Five-a-side & Volleys		Evening		
Fitness			Other		

Thursday

Football activity		Hours	Other physical activities		Hours
Club			School	Basketball	
School			After-school		1
Match			Evening	Cross-country	1
Fitness			Other		

Friday		Hours				Hours
Club				School		
School				After-school	Gym	1
Match				Evening		
Fitness				Other		

Saturday		Hours				Hours
Club				School		
School	Training	1.5		After-school		
Match	Team shape & free kicks			Evening		
Fitness				Other		

Sunday		Hours				Hours
Club				School		
School	Match vs. Bromley FC	1.5		After-school		
Match				Evening		
Fitness				Other		
		7				**4**

Main weekly targets and objectives

This week I am working on	Improving my left foot
I need to improve this because	am not much good on my left!
And when I achieve this it would mean	I can play better & shoot more with my left like Thierry Henry
I use self-talk by continually telling myself (see Chapter 3)	I can do it! I keep reminding myself to concentrate
I use imagery by seeing myself (see Chapter 8)	Playing great passes
I focused by	Clenching my fist when the ball went out
I am using my routines to	Get ready when the ball goes dead

Summary

- **Develop a player-centred approach to your coaching.**

- **Develop a player-first, winning-second approach.**

- **Keep communication lines open with all of your players.**

- **Set time aside to talk with your players.**

- **Get to know things about your players outside of football.**

Self testers

1　Why do young players play football?
2　Why is it important to get to know your players, and how can you do this?
3　What are the benefits of players completing a weekly diary?

Action plan

Get to know your players　During the next month, get all of the squad to identify their reasons for participation. They can fill in a small questionnaire or feed back in small groups. Keep a record of this. In addition, develop player information sheets to enable you to get to know all of your players' likes and dislikes. Encourage players to be as honest as possible when completing the questionnaires and giving feedback. If you take the same group next season, carry out the same exercise to see if their reasons for participation have changed.

Chapter 2

Motivation

> THIS CHAPTER WILL:
> - Help you to understand what motivation really is.
> - Explore differences between trying to do your best and trying to win.
> - Describe how to create an optimal training environment to motivate players.
> - Explain how you can motivate your players.
> - Offer suggestions on how to motivate players at training and on match days.

Along with confidence, motivation is one of the most overused and probably least understood terms in football.

'The player's not motivated!', 'He's not trying hard enough!', and 'She doesn't want it enough!' These are phrases often spoken by frustrated team managers and coaches standing on the side of the pitch during training and matches every week. Motivation is often confused with being 'psyched up', and in this chapter we will discuss the differences between these terms. In particular, we will look at some simple ways of motivating your players.

What is motivation?

Motivation is influenced by two concepts, importance and confidence. Players and teams apparently lacking in motivation could be asked: 'How great is your desire to achieve?' (importance) and 'How optimistic are you about being able to achieve your target?' (confidence). A player lacking the desire will be hard to motivate. Equally, a player with desire but lacking confidence could be just as difficult to motivate. 'What's the point in trying? . . . I can't do it anyway' may well be the attitude.

To understand what motivates a player, we should remember the reasons for participating in football in the first place (see Chapter 1). Coaches should strive to understand each player's personal motives since this will significantly affect attitudes, enjoyment and performance. The environment in which coaching takes place can also affect a player's motivation, and it is a challenge for the coach to create as positive an environment as possible.

Quote | 'You can motivate players better with kind words than you can with a whip.'

Don't confuse motivation and psyching up. Inexperienced coaches believe motivation is about giving a tough pre-match or half-time speech to get players going. While this may, on the face of it, appear to be a good ploy on occasions, the disadvantages of consistently using this approach will far outweigh any advantage. Over-psyching can be as big a problem as being too relaxed. If you want your players to perform to their maximum, to carry out instructions and concentrate on the team strategy and their own game plan, better they are relaxed before going onto the pitch, than in a frenzy. To help achieve the optimum motivation for your players, you need to understand and appreciate them as individuals. Some may need a quiet word before going out and playing;

others may prefer to be left alone for a couple of minutes so they can concentrate on their own game plan.

Statistic
There are over 14,000 coaches registered with The FA's Coaches Association.

Typical definitions of motivation refer to the direction and intensity of effort. It is the reason why people choose to do some things and why they avoid other things.

Motivation involves several factors; personality of the individual (genetic), social variables (environmental), thoughts that come into play when a person undertakes a task at which he or she is evaluated (for example, being watched by the coach or by teammates), competition with others (a match), or attempting to attain some standard of excellence.

There are two main types of motivation – intrinsic and extrinsic.

Intrinsic motivation
Intrinsic behaviour refers to activities that are performed for internal reasons, for example – the enjoyment, pleasure and satisfaction inherent in the activity. This form of motivation is likely to occur when the activity is interesting, challenging and provides players with clear feedback and freedom with which to perform the task. It is sometimes referred to as self-motivation. It is the reason most young players start playing football in the first place. It's fun! It is also a key ingredient for high achievers and top players.

Being intrinsically motivated leads individuals to experience pleasant emotions and to feel free and relaxed. They experience little pressure or tension, and they are focused on the task. Because of this, coaches should strive to make activities and practices functional and fun. For

instance, why not ask players what they would really like to do in a session and set some time aside for their requests each month? This could involve different activities for different players, and so may require more coaches to help supervise and offer positive feedback.

Best Practice Make sessions interesting and challenging. Provide players with clear feedback. Allow players freedom to perform the task and learn from it. Encourage players to help set some of the content for some sessions.

Extrinsic motivation

Extrinsic behaviour refers to activities that are performed for external reasons, for example, to seek popularity from friends or because it pleases parents, or playing football for another reason such as receiving rewards (medals, trophies, money) or avoiding punishment (or a negative consequence, for example, parents moaning). Extrinsic motivation refers to engaging in an activity as a means to an end and not for its own sake; individuals seek to obtain social and material rewards from participation. This form of motivation can lead players to feel tensed, pressurized and nervous as the achievement of rewards is not under total control of the player. Social approval, for example, depends on others and is outside our control.

■ Refer back to the task in Chapter 1 where you asked players why they play football (p. 6). How many gave intrinsic motives and how many gave extrinsic motives for playing?

Comparisons to teammates or to yourself

One important aspect of motivation is an understanding of why a player trains or participates in football. This sounds simple but the implications are crucial in terms of player development.

Quote | 'Winning doesn't always mean being first. Winning means you're doing better than you've ever done before.'

Ego orientation

If a player's sole objective in training is to show that he or she is better than other players, or to always win, this is known as an ego orientation. Players with ego orientation tend to feel more tense and anxious in competitive situations unless they are totally confident about beating their opponent. This is the same for both training and match situations. Ego-orientated players may be more likely to demonstrate poor behaviour in sessions and matches such as blaming others, moaning, and sometimes even cheating. They are less likely to accept coach criticism (particularly in front of their peers), and tend to give up more easily when compared to a task-orientated player.

Task orientation

Task orientation refers to a player's inclination towards the mastery of a situation; a player trying to learn or improve a skill, regardless of what teammates can do, shows a task orientation. These types of player generally persist longer, select more challenging tasks, and enjoy themselves more than ego-orientated players. This is not to say that players should not strive to be winners. It is simply a matter of putting the two situations in perspective and prioritizing your attitude. Concentrate on the task, and the performance will take care of itself. Win or lose, you will generally get the best from your players when emphasizing a task orientation.

A simple example of the impact of task and ego orientation would be two players (Player A and Player B) taking part in a group race. Player A simply wants to win the race and will put the minimum effort in to do so. If he/she is much faster than the rest, he/she does not have to exert tremendous effort. If he/she feels they may not win, he/she simply gives up. Normally with an excuse! Player B, however, continually strives to achieve a personal best (PB). Regardless of where he or she is in the race, his/her objective remains the same – to improve his/her own PB. Player B is more likely to improve over time, exert greater effort and persist. He or she is also likely to enjoy the experience of competing and does not take defeat as badly as Player A, especially as his/her PB is improved.

   Over the next four training sessions, really observe players and see which players are more task orientated and which are more ego orientated. Develop a strategy with other staff to make players concentrate on the quality of their own performance, irrespective of the outcome.

Creating the optimal environment to motivate your players

Motivating individuals

One thing all successful coaches and managers find out quickly is that players do not care what you, the coach/manager, knows until they know you care (as mentioned in Chapter 1). It is important not only to let players know you care, you must show them! One of the most effective ways to do this is to take an interest in a player when they are injured and so not at training. Ring them up and keep in contact. Show you care.

Motivating your team

Highly motivated teams are generally more successful and satisfied, and persist in the face of failure and choose more challenging options than less motivated teams. Motivating the team involves creating the right environment. It is an everyday thing. An every session thing. One of the most useful models to use for creating an effective motivational environment is the TARGET model described in Table 5. Essentially,

TARGET can be used to enhance individual and team motivation and it breaks a session down into six key elements:

- **Task.**
- **Authority.**
- **Recognition.**
- **Grouping.**
- **Evaluation.**
- **Time.**

Task

When selecting drills and practices, coaches should consider many elements, including:

- The ability of the players.
- The different abilities between players.
- The different player-position requirements (e.g. goalkeeper).
- The time of the season.
- When the practice takes place during the training session.

If players succeed in challenging drills, they will feel really confident. Therefore, don't make the drills too simple. Likewise, if players are unsuccessful this can have a reverse effect and knock their confidence. Your practice design needs to be considered in some detail – it is an art to get it right. Players enjoy variety; this keeps them stimulated and helps maintain a fun element. So, vary your practices within a training session, and from week to week. Keep any individual practice within the whole session short (15–20 minutes) and then move on to something else. Try and interlink the practices to ensure some continuity and progress between them. For example, a simple passing drill (Practice 1) may

Table 5 **TARGET: Ways of creating a mastery motivational climate**

Creating a positive motivational climate	Strategies
Task: Coaching activities	• Include variety and individually challenging activities. • Encourage players to focus on the task not the outcome. • Emphasize enjoyment.
Authority: How the coach operates and communicates with the players	• Let players have a say in matters. • Encourage problem solving. • Use a democratic coaching style whenever possible.
Recognition: What is rewarded	• Recognize personal progress and improvement in players.
Grouping: Use of groups	• Be flexible over groupings in practice. • Be careful when having the most skilled or least skilled players together. • Encourage group problem solving.
Evaluation: Use of feedback	• Evaluation based on improvement and effort. • Allow players to evaluate themselves as well as be evaluated by others. • Be careful with public evaluation.
Time: Scheduling	• Allow time for practice and improvement. • Help players with time management to encourage practice.

progress to a 3 vs. 1 passing session (Practice 2) and then into a possession game 8 vs. 4 (Practice 3) and so on.

Best Practice Emphasize personal improvement with players concentrating on their own performance. Emphasize enjoyment. Don't make it too serious!

Authority

You don't have to use a style of coaching that shouts orders out and directs players where they should be, what they should be doing and when they should be doing it! Set up the practice and let the players play. Allow them to make decisions. Remember that children are not mini-adults and should be treated accordingly.

Best Practice Mistakes enhance learning, so offer constructive feedback (see Chapter 6) without being critical or sarcastic. Let players have some say in the session and do not be afraid to ask for their opinions.

Recognition

Be a positive coach and recognize when players do well. It may be a case of keeping quiet while things are not going quite as well as they should be, and then being vocal and giving encouragement and praise when your player does something right. Recognition need not be a tangible reward such as a medal.

Best Practice Genuine praise and encouragement can be more effective in creating a positive environment than tangible rewards.

Grouping

The way you group players can and will affect the level of motivation. It may be useful to occasionally devise practices for the goalkeepers, defenders, mid-field and attackers separately so that they develop pride in their 'sub-unit', and can train without having to compare themselves to others in different groups. Usually players of similar abilities will be grouped together so that practices flow better and players can encourage each other. It can also be useful to use mixed-ability groups sometimes. This can have the effect of motivating the player of lesser ability to try harder, and allows the better ability player to concentrate on self-improvement (rather than social comparison). The message is to be flexible and don't be afraid to try different groups and different practices.

Evaluation

Related to recognition, evaluation involves giving feedback to players on their personal improvement and effort. Evaluation is how you assess players during sessions. You can also be flexible here and ask players to give their own assessment, for instance, ask 'How do you think that went?'. In this way, the player has to think about his or her own performance and offer an opinion. Moreover, ask players to give each other feedback. This can further help their development because they start to think more about how they carry out instructions.

Time

Plan your sessions and generally stick to the times allocated for each practice. You may need to extend practices sometimes to emphasize points or to allow time for more improvement for most players. However, don't extend practices to the detriment of the overall session or until the rest of the players become bored if one player does not progress as quickly. In this instance, you may pull out the player for extra attention (staff permitting) or set homework for a player that needs to practice a particular skill that others have perfected.

Best Practice Use the TARGET model to create an optimum training environment.

Motivating your team to train!

One of the easiest ways to help motivate your players to train is to provide them with interesting, progressively challenging and varied forms of practice. If players turn up for training and see an array of fluorescent cones and poles set out, bibs and balls ready, drinks and first aid prepared, you can often sense the anticipation – 'What's coach got lined up for us today?'. Compare this to players turning up for training only to find that coach is late – 'OK . . . off around the pitch three times while I get things ready'. You probably get the picture.

Best Practice You will generally find that the better prepared you are as a coach, the more the players will enjoy the session. Simple really.

■   Over the next two weeks, allow players some say in training sessions and be flexible enough to change when things are not quite going to plan.

Motivating the team on match day

On match day players are looking forward to emulating their idols. Great ways to keep players highly motivated on match days include:

- If you can get to the ground early and set the kit out on pegs, it makes the players feel extra special when they arrive.
- Make sure all the balls, first aid and refreshments are prepared before players arrive.
- Develop a flexible range of timed warm-ups and be prepared to be flexible.
- Set goals for the players.
- Do not get players too hyped up before the start of the game.
- Let players know that they are free to make mistakes and try the things they have been practising in training.

- **Do not continually shout out instructions throughout the game. Trust players to do their best – they will learn by making their own decisions.**
- **Set guidelines for parent behaviour (see Chapter 9).**

■ Arrange a meeting every month where all key staff discuss and have an input into the training and match-day schedules. Encourage everyone to be open and honest and to speak out!

Setting specific match objectives is a useful way to focus players' minds on the game. Just before going out, ask them to sit down and think about the game in their mind's eye and to think of the things they wish to achieve (see Chapter 8).

Team motivation indicator

Many coaches assess the morale of their substitutes and squad players in order to determine whether the team as a whole is motivated (we make the assumption here that 'team' refers to starting players only, whilst 'squad' refers to all members of the group). Generally, if the last substitute has good morale then the squad as a whole will be more cohesive (stay together and work for each other). This is a good indicator of team morale and motivation. At the top level, Ferguson, Wenger and Ranieri have issues with large squads, and constantly work to develop a squad standard. This does not mean that the substitutes have to be happy at not playing, simply that they appreciate that their input is important within the structure of the team.

Team strengths and areas for improvement

It is useful to ask players their opinions on the team's strengths and areas for improvement, and to compare these thoughts to your own list. This can lead to discussions with the players and is a means of getting players to focus on their perceived strengths during games, while focusing on developing their perceived weaknesses during training.

■   Arrange a team meeting for players to discuss team issues. Ask players to complete a 'team strengths and areas for improvement' sheet as shown in Table 6 (or similar). The replies can be summarized and used as the basis of the next meeting or for immediate discussion.

Players are not often asked for their opinions regarding the team performances. This is a shame because although the coach may not agree with all that is said, players will feel better for being asked. If only one positive thing comes out of the meeting that you can then put into practice, it may have big consequences in your team development and performance.

Best Practice Be confident and ask players their opinions. Be willing to listen to players. Be wiling to put some player ideas into practice.

Psychological needs of players

Players have three basic psychological needs that, when fulfilled, will lead to enhanced motivation:

1   To show that they have ability.
2   To feel they belong to the group.
3   To feel that they have an element of choice in doing what they are doing within the team (or with respect to their role within the team).

Table 6 **Team strengths and areas for improvement**

Team strengths and areas for improvement
Objective(s)
To discuss the team strengths and areas for improvement, to clarify the
interaction between each unit, to improve the awareness and understanding on
the pitch, and ultimately **improve individual and team performance**.

Strengths	Areas for improvement
1	1
2	2
3	3
4	4
5	5
6	6
7	7
8	8
9	9
10	10

Unit strengths/Areas for improvement
Goalkeepers/Defence/Mid-field/Attack

1	1
2	2
3	3
4	4
5	5
6	6
7	7
8	8

Ability

- From a very early age, players have a tremendous ability to learn.
- They are naturally inquisitive and curious, and enjoy exploring different ways of doing things.
- Young football players left alone will quite happily play keep-ups, practise volleys and headers.
- Players may simply put items of clothes down for goalposts and play the game.
- They will learn how to dribble, shoot, pass and tackle without instruction from adults.

As young players grow, they develop a desire to show others how good they are, how much ability they have at carrying out a task. Players want to demonstrate their ability to the coach, their parents, peers (friends), and even to themselves. An often neglected aspect of developing player ability is the fact that if players cannot 'demonstrate' how good they are (even from a self-referenced perspective), their motivation may be reduced to the point that they simply drop out of sport.

The implication for coaches is to:

- Make sure players have plenty of opportunity to succeed.
- Challenge your players (and yourself) to develop progressive practices that, on successful completion, will enhance the players' levels of competence.

Be flexible and don't be afraid to reduce/increase the level of expectancy and to make drills or practices easier/harder if need be; this ensures that player ability will be enhanced.

The way players are grouped is also important. Varying grouping can help players in different ways. Grouping similar-ability players can help development when players can see that they have similar ability to others (be careful that this does not lead to an increase in ego orientation). Mixed-ability grouping can often help by minimizing social comparison and players may concentrate on the tasks they are doing rather than on comparing themselves with others.

The quality of the training sessions, rather than quantity of training, is the key element here.

Best Practice Ensure players can succeed in the challenges you give them. The more success players achieve, the more confident they become. The more confident they become, the more they are motivated to persist. Give players plenty of positive feedback to emphasize how well they are doing. Be creative and progressive in the way you set up practices.

Coaches need to get to know the individual player.

If fun and enjoyment are key reasons for young players participating in sport then the more the coach can do to promote a positive experience the better.

The ability to handle pressure depends on a player's self-confidence.

Good coaches allow players to have a say in their own development and recognize that feedback is a two-way concept.

One of the easiest ways to help motivate your players to train is to provide them with interesting, challenging and varied forms of practice.

Players have to be aware of their specific role in the side.

Relationships within the club

Players need to feel accepted and respected by their peers and by their coach. They need to feel supported and very much part of the team (see Chapter 9). Let players know when they get it right. Offer plenty of positive feedback and try to minimize continual correction.

Best Practice Ensure you show players that you care about them as individuals. Treat all players with the same respect, especially non-starters (squad members not in the starting team). Do not exclude players from team practices without clear reasons and explanations.

The player's choice

Players like to know they are playing football because they want to, not simply because their parents want them to. They also want some choice in the activity they are doing. Players are much more likely to be motivated in an activity they have chosen. This does not imply letting the players run the sessions! But if you set up a session and ask players for their opinion on part of that session, or simply discuss with them and agree on a session plan, you'll be pleasantly surprised how they become more motivated over time. Remember, it is *their* training time, *their* fun time.

Best Practice Allow players to have some say in their training sessions. Discuss training strategies with the team and allow the players to have some input. Remember, playing football is your players' fun time.

Summary

- Players can be intrinsically or extrinsically motivated, or both.

- Players may have a task or ego orientation, or both.

- A task climate should be developed to maximize learning and development.

- Players are motivated when the task closely matches their ability.

- Progressive, varied, challenging and fun practices will help motivate your players.

- Preparation is essential to maintain motivation.

Self testers

1 Name two types of motivation.
2 What is the difference between ego and task orientation?
3 What is the TARGET model for motivating groups?

Action Plan

TARGET programme   Develop a monthly training programme using the principles of the TARGET motivational model. Ensure you use a variety of practices that progress to challenge your players. Ask the players to give suggestions about what they would like to work on.

Chapter 3

Confidence

THIS CHAPTER WILL:
- Describe what confidence really is.
- Explain why confidence is important.
- Explore ways to help players build their confidence.
- Explain how a coach can breed confidence.
- Describe a confidence climate.
- Explain how to create a training environment to help improve players' confidence.
- Describe how to help players' confidence on match day.

What is confidence?

Confidence is a much used term, and many say it is the most important factor in football enjoyment and performance. But what exactly is it? In football, self-confidence is often used to refer to a positive attitude and healthy belief in yourself and your football ability. It is the belief that you can successfully perform a given behaviour or task. This situation-specific self-confidence is known as self-efficacy. A football player may have a high degree of self-confidence in dribbling but a low degree of self-confidence in shooting.

Why is confidence important?

Self-confidence is the belief that you can perform a desired behaviour, and so a player's expectations of doing something will play a critical part in whether he/she achieves it or not. For example, a player confident in volleying a ball will not hesitate when a cross comes in at the right height and speed to take it first touch, on the volley. A less confident player may attempt to first control the ball, losing valuable seconds and perhaps even the opportunity to shoot.

Benefits of confidence

- Confidence gives you positive feelings – when you feel confident you are more likely to remain calm and relaxed under pressure. Footballers with higher levels of self-confidence will experience less anxiety at the same stress level as a footballer with lower self-confidence.

- Confidence allows concentration – when you feel confident your mind is freed and can focus on what is necessary to play well.

- Confidence encourages you to stretch yourself, to 'reach higher' – confident people tend to set goals and face challenges in which there is a high degree of uncertainty concerning the outcome, and pursue them with more vigour. People who are not confident either set goals which are easy to achieve or which are too difficult to achieve. These players will be content to play teams or go one on one against others who are either much less able than them or who are much better, so in effect minimizing the challenge faced.

- Confidence encourages effort and persistence – confident players will often work harder and persist for longer, especially under adverse conditions. Football players with low self-confidence tend to show low levels of effort in striving to achieve a task. When faced with difficult situations (for instance, prolonged lack of success, tough opponents, the match score against them), their 'heads go down' more quickly (i.e. players get demoralized and discouraged). Confidence allows you to be a rubber ball in that it allows you to bounce back from set-backs!

- Confidence affects the way players play – confident players tend to play to win, in that they want the ball, are not afraid to take chances, and take control of the match. However, players lacking in confidence tend to play not to lose – they play cautiously and try to avoid making mistakes and often avoid touching the ball altogether!

▓ Think of your most confident player. Make a list of all the mental qualities that this player possesses such as focus, motivation, calm under pressure and so forth.

Building confidence

Many people believe that you either have confidence or you don't. The fact is that the confidence of a young player is the sum of all the thoughts they have about themselves as a football player. Coaches and parents can play a significant role in developing the self-confidence of the player.

There are four areas of confidence that we can explore:

- **Success breeds confidence.**
- **The 'If they can do it I can' phenomenon.**
- **The voices you hear.**
- **Going to acting school – acting 'As if . . .'.**

Two effective questions a coach can ask a player to gain more information about these four areas of confidence are:

1   **'What gives you confidence and where do you get it from?'**
2   **'What knocks your confidence and what takes it away?'**

Success breeds confidence

The phrase 'success breeds success' is well-known and accepted in football. The phrase more accurately could be 'success breeds confidence and confidence breeds success, and so on'.

Examples where you could bring this point to life include:

- Waiting for the success to come along, whether it is a good pass, a timely tackle, a session in which the player has worked very hard, and so forth, and then praising it.

- **Providing more positive feedback than negative.**
- **Reminding players of their past successes – encouraging them to keep a 'success file'.**

At your next training session, try and make a mental note of how much genuine positive feedback you give to players. Try and include some information with the feedback, for example:

'Well done Jody, great body shape and good balance on that volley.'

or

'Fantastic Ben, terrific running back after we lost possession!'

Quote | 'Catch them doing well and tell them!'

Success, however, does not just happen. There is no substitute for hard work and thorough preparation as this quote from David Calleja, a high-level swimming coach and Great Britain Coach of the Year Award winner shows: (quoted from *Coaching Focus*, 1997)

Quote | 'The ability to handle pressure depends on a player's self-confidence. In competition, confidence comes from the knowledge that preparation has been as thorough as possible – everything that could be done, has been done. It is only if athletes doubt their preparation that they will doubt their ability to deliver. The seeds of anxiety are sown in the cracks this leaves in their confidence.'

Creating a confidence climate

The nature of the environment in which a young football player trains and plays matches is vitally important if a player is to develop their self-confidence and grow as a person as well as a football player. By its very nature, football will try to drain a young football player of his or her confidence. During every practice session and match, even the best players will make some poor passes, miss shots or miss tackles. All but the top teams in their league will lose more matches than they will win. Therefore, maintaining confidence, never mind increasing it, is like a salmon swimming upstream. You have to work hard to stay where you are. If we compare the climate in which the young player practises and competes in football to the weather, most of us would feel better on a sunny warm day where the people we see around us are positive, having fun and are smiling, rather than a dull, cold, rainy day where people are negative and critical. So what can you do?

Quote | 'Put some **sunshine** into the players' football!'

Developing beliefs

We think and behave in a way that supports and reinforces our beliefs. Expectations of the player are critical in determining whether players reach their potential or not.

These expectations and beliefs are often ingrained by the expectations and beliefs of significant others such as parents and coaches.

Be aware of your own expectations of the player – are they too high or too low? A coach will give 'high expectation' players more instructional and informational feedback. Moreover, a coach will generally provide more reinforcement and praise for high-expectation players after a successful performance. Coaches who have a low expectation of what a player can do will expect a lower standard of performance from them, and will invariably get it! This is because they inadvertently put a negative self-fulfilling prophecy on the player.

Statistic

Darwen, who lost 18 in a row in the 1898–99 season, hold the record for the worst losing streak in English League football.

Here are some general guidelines to 'coaching confidence':

- **Feedback to be positive.** When players are young and still learning the skills of the game, they will make more mistakes than have successes, and so it is important to be patient as a coach or parent and wait for the 'good stuff'. It is often what is *not* said as a coach that is more important than what is said.

- Make your feedback expressive – use superlatives rather than 'good' or 'well done'. For example, you might offer feedback to a player who has just made a long run and finished with a poor pass: 'Terrific run James, relax on the pass next time, and keep making those great runs!'

- Use the feedback phrase of 'That's unlike you not to . . .'. For example, 'That's unlike you not to track back' or 'That's unlike you not to win those headers' or 'That's unlike you to give up when we're losing.'

- Change the drills and exercises in the session after the players have achieved some specific success.

- Reduce the 'but' and increase the 'and'. For instance, after the coach has seen a player dribble past two players and shoot when it would have been better to pass because they became overly excited, the coach might say, 'Great dribble, but next time if you look up you may see the pass.' Alternatively the coach could say, 'Great dribble, and next time if you look up you may see the pass.' The only word change is the substitution of 'but' with 'and'. It is often said that using the word 'but' cancels out everything that went before it. Using 'and' maintains the positive nature of the first part of the feedback and ensures that the instructional part of the feedback is perceived as positive rather than slightly critical.

- Use the word 'don't' very sparingly in your sessions! Try to use the more positive word 'do' instead. Tell players what you want and how they can do it, rather than what you don't want and how they shouldn't do it.

- You can coach confidence.
- The coach's own belief in the person's ability to change becomes a self-fulfilling prophecy.

The '*If they can do it I can*' phenomenon: look, learn, and get more confident

Players can gain self-confidence from watching someone, usually of similar ability, successfully perform an action. To illustrate, a young football player may gain self-confidence to perform ten keep-ups after having seen their friend achieve the same, since they believe they are of similar ability. If a team member attends a trial and is selected, that may give the other players in the team confidence that they can do the same.

■ The 'Catch-22'

A team has lost their last five matches and is languishing at the bottom of the table. Team coach: 'We just need to start winning then we'll have more belief in ourselves!' So now what? Without winning the team has very little confidence, and with low confidence the team has very little chance of winning, and so on.

List the ways in which you could increase the confidence of the team, which in turn will increase their chances of winning, and if they do win will significantly increase their confidence.

The voices you hear

Self-confidence is about believing in your own ability. Consequently, ways of encouraging positive thinking and the use of positive statements to describe a player can be extremely effective ways of giving confidence. Our brain is like a radio receiver – it receives thousands of signals every day. These signals or the thoughts we have every day are

usually either negative or positive. This 'self-talk', that 'little voice' inside your head, is rarely neutral. It is often said that a player's confidence is the sum of all the thoughts they have about themself as a player.

In order to perform consistently, a football player has to think positively and consistently. The voices that you hear come from two main sources:

1   Yourself – otherwise known as self-talk.

2   Others – in the form of verbal persuasion or feedback from significant others, e.g. parents, family, coaches and peers.

Best Practice Wait for the positive behaviours to come along and feed back on them. It is often said that children receive more negative feedback than positive! Give individual feedback and try to make it specific.

▨   Ask players to come up with a short and catchy personal statement. It should be written in a positive way in the present tense. Examples would include: 'I always bounce back from a set-back', 'I am an agile and tenacious defender who attacks the ball'.

The statement should contain 'hot' words, that is to say, words which have emotional meaning for the person. Sit with the player and personalize the affirmation using their words.

The link between self-confidence and the reasons people give for success and failure

If how we think can ultimately affect our self-confidence, a greater understanding of how people explain their successes and failures, and how we can retrain their thinking if it is not conducive to them becoming a more effective sportsperson, is crucial if we are to help increase a player's self-confidence.

Players with high self-confidence have been found to explain failure with a lack of effort, while players with low self-confidence tend to offer lack of ability as a reason for the failure. Self-confident players explain success as coming from themselves (internal), as a result of their ability, which is seen as being fairly permanent or stable and as a result of something that is under their control, for example, their match tactics.

If, after a poor performance, the coach attributes the reason for the performance to poor effort as opposed to a lack of ability, the players' belief in themselves will remain intact and may even increase!

Asking confidence-building questions

Another way to encourage players to talk positively to themselves is to ask them questions that will encourage answers of a positive and confidence-building nature. For example, consider the nature of the answers to these confidence-building questions:

*   'What personal strengths do you have that will help you to succeed?'
*   'When are you a really good football player?'
*   'What gives you some confidence that you can do this?'
*   'Is there anything else you can think of that would help you feel more confident?'

Best Practice Encourage players to manage their self-talk. Encourage them to build up a library of positive talk. In order for players to perform positively, they have to think positively.

Going to acting school – acting 'As if . . .

The mind–body link is often represented as:

Thoughts → Feeling → Behaviours

How you think influences how you feel, which in turn influences how you behave or what you do.

It often helps players to 'act as if . . .', once they understand that performing at football is similar to being an actor. They can have a 'performer' self and a 'real' self. The performer self can switch on as soon as the training or match starts, rather like the actor who takes on the characteristics, behaviours and attitudes of a role when the director shouts, 'and action!'

Performer self and the real self

What is the script in sport and football? What words would stand out in that script about 'how you need to be' as a player? Before a player goes out on the pitch, try asking the question 'How do you want to be on the pitch today?', rather than 'What do you want to do on the pitch today?'

Coach/Parent: What do you want to do in the match today?

Player: I want to have a good first touch and spread the ball wide at every opportunity.

or

Coach: How do you want to be in the match today?

Player: I want to be lively, positive and calmly aggressive.

Quote | 'The more a football player acts confidently, the more likely they are to feel confident.'

Confidence in what?

As we have already said, self-confidence is significantly influenced by success. Success, however, can mean different things to different people. What is failure for one person may be success for another.

▨ Write down what success looks like for you as a coach of football players or for you as a parent of your football-playing child.

Some people judge success as outperforming others, beating others, being selected for example, ahead of others, being ranked above others and so forth. The problem with this is that if the player or team starts to lose or believes that future success in their terms is unlikely, their confidence will fall. It is therefore important that a player has a high level of task orientation as mentioned in Chapter 2. Here, confidence is associated with a player's own personal improvement, with effort and to the performance rather than the result. All of these are significantly within the control of the player, and so he or she can approach achieving them with a greater sense of confidence.

Coaches, parents and players who judge success in terms of their own improvement and 'getting the better of the sport' will have self-confidence that is resilient because it is more resistant to losses and failures which we know are part and parcel of football. Confidence will be maintained as long as the person believes that personal improvements will continue. Sports such as athletics, swimming and gymnastics, in which performance can be measured with actual numbers (for instance, time taken to run 800 m, distance jumped in the long jump, time for 50 m backstroke and score on the parallel bars), have an advantage over football in that one can come second or last but still achieve a personal best. This is somewhat harder to achieve in football because individual performance is not so easily measured. Nevertheless, this should not deter coaches from striving to establish and quantify personal best (PB) performances for their players.

If self-confidence is linked to the expectation of doing something and people have more self-confidence of things they feel they have control over, consider whether a young football player would have more confidence of winning a match or trying really hard in the match to prevent all but one cross and make at least four overlaps as a left-back? If the environment in which the young football player can practice and compete is one where coaches and parents help to encourage them to act in a task or 'performance-emphasized' way (see Table 7), then they may grow into confident, motivated football players, who love the game.

■ Consider the effects on the behaviour and thinking of a young football player playing football in the two contrasting environments shown in Table 7.

Table 7 **Winning and performance**

Winning emphasized	Performance emphasized
An environment where 'to win' means 'to beat'	'To win' means to try hard
Players are compared to one another	Learning and personal progress is valued and emphasized
Mistakes are punished (negative consequence)	Mistakes are seen as part of learning
Showing superior ability over others is emphasized and rewarded	Effort is rewarded
Players are told what to do	Choice is allowed and nurtured

Quote | 'Even when things are going wrong I have the will to win. Let's say that when times are bad I am able to act as though they are good, and when things are going well I am also able to bear in mind that there will be dodgy times ahead at some point or other.'
David Trezeguet, Juventus and France

Consider the following behaviours and thoughts from young football players and reflect upon which environment they might be connected to:

- 'I feel safe enough to take some risks and actually feel as though the coach wants me to experiment with my skills.'

- 'I like it when my Mum and Dad smile and encourage me when I try a trick and it doesn't quite come off.'
- 'I feel a bit down when the coach tells me that I'll be better when I can cross the ball like Andy.'
- 'Mum, Dad, I won the 'most improved player of the week' T-shirt for this week.'
- 'We got beaten today and the coach wasn't happy!'
- 'Dad, I really like my football training because we also get to say what we want to do . . .'
- 'My Mum and Dad just seem to want me to try hard and have lots of fun.'
- 'Players give up when they are 3–0 down and think they cannot win.'

Best Practice Parents and coaches should strive to create a positive, confidence-building environment where mistakes are seen as a vital part of learning, and personal progress is emphasized. The individual should be valued and have freedom of choice.

Summary

- **Confidence can be developed.**

- **Catch players doing things well and praise them.**

- **Give genuine, positive feedback with information.**

- **Affirmation statements are a great way to remind players of their strengths.**

Self testers

1 Why is confidence important and what strategies can I use to enhance confidence?

2 List four things that can help build confidence in a player.

3 What type of feedback is best to enhance confidence, and when would you use it?

Action plan

Building confidence Set some goals over the next four weeks, to enhance confidence. Develop a strategy outline for all coaches at the club on creating a playing environment (both for training and matches) that will help to build confidence. Include a list of do's and dont's.

Chapter 4

Team spirit and team building

THIS CHAPTER WILL:
- Offer ideas to help you to develop team spirit.
- Explain the importance of players understanding their roles within the team.
- Introduce ideas for team meetings.
- Explore how you can develop a close team by using mission statements and team anthems.

Quote

'Teamwork isn't simple. In fact it can be a frustrating and elusive commodity. That's why there are so many bad teams out there, stuck in neutral or going downhill. Teamwork doesn't appear magically, just because someone mouths the words. It doesn't thrive just because of the presence of talent or ambition. It doesn't flourish simply because the team has tasted success.'
Pat Riley, *The Winner Within*, 1993

The most important person when considering sport in general, and sport psychology in particular, is the individual player. However, football is a team game, and managers and coaches are forever trying to mould a group of individuals into a successful and cohesive unit. The quotation on the previous page from American coach, Pat Riley, sums up the fact that it is not easy to build a successful team. How do you ensure that you have the right blend of players in your team? How do you get that chemistry right? Harder still, how do you get squad chemistry right when some players are hardly playing?

Developing team spirit

We have already discussed ways in which a team can be motivated to succeed (Chapter 2) and how to create the confidence in their ability to succeed (Chapter 3). Successful teams will also use SMARTER goal-setting in both the long and the short term (Chapter 7). Moreover, good leadership and communication skills are essential elements in team building. In this chapter we will discuss specific ways in which team spirit can be enhanced, and we shall look at various team-building exercises.

It is worth considering the fact that successful companies and teams do not have a secret formula. They do not do one or two things right to achieve success. They do many small things, every day. They do not do things right once in a while, they do them right every time. A quote from another American coach, John Wooden, sums it up well:

| Quote | 'If you keep too busy learning the tricks of the trade, you may never learn the trade.' John Wooden in *Beyond Winning*, G. M. Walton, 1992 |

Team building involves doing many small things right. It takes leading by example. It takes, as the England World Cup winning rugby coach, Clive Woodward, says:

Quote | 'Preparation, preparation, preparation.'

Team building, in the same way as team motivation, is concerned with creating the right environment for players to develop 'free of fear'.

Best Practice It is the whole environment that you create, and what you, your staff and the parents do and say every day, that will encourage team spirit to grow.

Components that can help create team spirit

• Good communication.

• Distinctiveness and identity.

• Team name.

• Team kit.

- Team mission statement.
- Team song.
- Understanding team roles.
- Developing pride within the different positions, e.g. mid-field.
- Setting challenging team goals.
- Discouraging criticism and sarcasm.
- Avoiding the formation of cliques.
- Using team meetings.
- Knowing something personal about each player.

Communication

An effective coach or manager will create an environment where players are happy to express their thoughts and feelings. Team building requires openness, trust and mutual respect between the player and coach. A democratic style of leadership will help in this regard (see Chapter 5 on Leadership and coaching).

Distinctiveness and identity

Distinctiveness is what makes your team unique. It makes the players feel special and feel that they belong. There are many ways in which a team can promote its distinctiveness to help build team spirit. Three such ways are in the team name, kit and mission statement.

Team name

Your team obviously has a name! In itself this will create a bond for the players. Many teams will use a nickname, something quite personal to them. This could be a normal club nickname (eagles, bees, lions and so on) or it could be made up by you and the players to epitomize what you are about. Personalized names help create distinctiveness which can help teams become more 'together'.

Team kit

The team kit gives players an identity. Teams that can afford tracksuits and matching bags look the part, and consequently this helps in the bonding process.

Team mission statement or team song

Ask your players to make up a positive mission statement that reflects what the team is all about. A typical example could be: 'We are a close team, who play together and work together. We have good values and train to the max!'

If you have musically talented players (or any good rappers!), you may even come up with a team song. A team song can be very powerful and emotive.

■ Think of a way in which you can make your team more distinctive. Give players a week to come up with ideas based on the team nickname for a team song or mission statement.

Team roles

Players have to be aware of their specific role within the side. These roles include the position within the team (forward, centre-back, goalkeeper and so on) and the responsibility, for example, captain, vice captain, midfield 'general' and so forth. A useful way of clarifying responsibilities is for the coach to list all the responsibilities a player has in a certain position, while asking players to do the same. It will be interesting to see the variations between each perspective. Once roles are clarified, it is important that they are agreed, understood and accepted by the player.

Acceptance is crucial. Parents should be made aware of individual player roles and responsibilities in order to avoid conflicting information being given to young players.

Quote | 'Team spirit is a competitive advantage.'

Develop pride within the different positions

The TARGET model was discussed earlier in relation to motivation (Chapter 2) and one of its elements is grouping. An important element in team building is to build PRIDE (Personal Responsibility In Developing Excellence) within the team. Players should feel proud playing for their team. One way to enhance this feeling of pride is to develop pride within the sub-units of defence (including the goalkeeper), mid-field and attack. In training, these units can be divided occasionally to carry out specific exercises for their area of the pitch. Specific goals can be set for each unit. In mid-field, for example, a goal can be set to not let any runners go past the mid-fielders without being tracked, and a set number of crosses must be achieved. Goal-setting will help focus the mind – not only of the individual, but also of the group. It will help create that 'We can do it' attitude.

Personal		**T**eam
Responsibility		**E**veryone
In	in the	**A**chieves
Developing		**M**ore
Excellence		

Set challenging team goals

Some managers do not like setting challenging goals because they define failure. Others set totally unrealistic goals (for instance, 'We won't lose a game!'). Setting realistic, specific and challenging team goals has a positive effect on individual and team performance. Goals set standards for the team and keep the team focused on what it needs to accomplish. Goals can also have a great effect in reducing any feelings of pressure or anxiety in players.

■ Set some challenging team goals with your players that can be achieved! For example, you might challenge players to make a sequence of five passes in a game.

Discourage criticism and sarcasm

Most teams will go through phases where arguments occur. This is natural and can help lead to progress and development if handled in the right way. However, forms of internal criticism and sarcasm should not be allowed to develop, let alone continue. What one or a few players deem as funny, others will perceive as insulting and disrespectful. Allowed to continue, this could be the quickest way to damage any work you have carried out to build team spirit.

Quote | 'Teamwork divides the task and doubles the success.'

Avoid the formation of cliques

Players often form cliques when the team is going through a poor run. Cliques tend to be disruptive to a team and should be discouraged. There will always be some players who are closer to each other than to other teammates. Nevertheless, when it comes to training and playing the team must be encouraged to become one. You can stop cliques forming, or becoming a negative influence, by splitting the players up to work in different groups or on different teams in training. Team discussions will help promote positive relationships and can make players aware of the negative effect of cliques and the need to foster mutual trust and belief.

Team meetings

Team meetings are underused in football and should be encouraged. They may be scheduled once a month or once every two months, and do not necessarily need to be more regular. They are essential if well run. This means that the meetings should be structured. A clear agenda must be set so that something specific is gained from the meeting. Meetings should run for a set time (not too long – 30 minutes should be adequate). Most importantly, players should be encouraged to express their opinions, and their concerns must be dealt with in the way you feel most appropriate. Having a meeting and not allowing players to talk, or worse still not taking on board any of their concerns, can make subsequent meetings nothing more than an exercise for the coach to show authority. No use for team development at all. Meetings are ideal for resolving internal conflicts, discussing training programmes, match strategies, and clarifying roles and responsibilities.

Quote | 'What to do with a mistake: Recognize it, admit it, learn from it, forget it.'

Know something personal about each player

In Chapter 1 there are some player information sheets (Tables 1 and 2) which include questions unrelated to football. These questions ask about favourite books, magazines and radio stations. There are also questions on family members and friends. Players feel special when a coach takes some time to talk to them about personal issues. It may be a simple, 'Have you read any more Harry Potter books?' to, 'How's your younger brother?' or, 'How's school?' – anything apart from football. It shows that you care and that you have made a special effort to know about their lives outside football. Players will appreciate it. So will parents!

This attitude is more likely to foster individual commitment to excellence from the players because they feel valued and understood.

As mentioned earlier, Liverpool manager Gerard Houllier often speaks about setting aside an hour a day simply to ensure that he speaks to all of his players. He feels that this is an essential part of building a relationship of openness and trust, which is essential to building successful and tight-knit teams.

Summary

- **Team spirit can be built.**

- **Develop a team identity (using kits, names, logos and anthems).**

- **Make sure players understand and accept their role within the team.**

- **Discourage criticism and sarcasm.**

- **Avoid the formation of cliques.**

- **Use regular team meetings to hear everyone's opinions.**

- **Know something personal about each player.**

- **Give all players some of your time.**

Self testers

1 How can you create a really distinctive team?

2 Why should players be aware of their specific role within the team?

3 How can you develop pride within different positions on the pitch (defence, mid-field, attack)?

Action plan

Identity parade   Over the next two months, come up with as many ideas as possible for a special and unique team identity. Ensure that all players have a say in this at a specially-called team meeting.

Chapter 5

Leadership and coaching

THIS CHAPTER WILL:
- Explain some basic principles of leadership.
- Help to improve your effectiveness as a leader.
- Explore how you can create a positive team culture for your players.

For the purposes of this chapter, the terms 'leadership' and 'coaching' will be used to mean similar actions or behaviours. For all practical purposes, coaching can be described as face-to-face leadership (Martens, 1987).

What is leadership?

Many adults decide to take up a coaching role in junior football either after finishing their playing career or because of their children's involvement in junior football. It is a big leap from playing or parenting to coaching. Sport coaching develops people through improving their performance. Essentially, once you become a coach you have to get things done through others. You can't play for the team, so you have to let your players play the game! Consequently, you will need to develop some new skills and knowledge to help you to become an effective coach and leader.

Excellent coaches and leaders give the team direction by having a vision of what can be done. This could be to develop skills, enjoy the game and play in a youth league. Coaches and leaders are also concerned with the football environment. They look not only at the physical environment, but also at the psychological and social environments. By examining the various aspects of the environment, they develop a good team culture. The ideal environment allows the player to have the maximum opportunity to achieve success and, thus, achieve team success. Coaching is face-to-face leadership where the coach brings together players with different talents, backgrounds, interests and levels of motivation (reasons for playing in the team). It is also a people business where communication skills are essential (Martens, 1987).

Quote | 'To succeed, do the best you can, where you are, with what you have.'

There are many definitions of leaders, but leadership is essentially the action of an individual to influence others towards set goals (Martens, 1987).

Qualities of effective leaders

There is no definitive list of leadership qualities, but there are some qualities that many successful coaches have in common. Coaches can develop these qualities as outlined by Martens (1987):

- **Empathy – this is where the coach understands how the other person feels and sees things from their perspective. Coaches need to know their players' needs, take time to communicate with them and be willing to help them (see Chapter 1).**
- Acting like leaders. Coaches are not 'one of the players'.
- Self-control. Coaches remain in control of their emotions when dealing with people (adults and children).
- Constantly striving to develop their own skills.
- Communicating positively with others.
- Flexiblility.

Leadership and coaching style

The coach's or leader's style is the tendency to lead the group or team in a particular way. This style often reflects their personality, knowledge and experience (Sports Coach UK, 2003). Traditionally the two most recognized styles are the autocratic and democratic. An autocratic coach makes decisions and tells people what to do. Democratic coaches share the situation or problem with other people and take into account their views before making a decision. Coaches often think they have to be one or the other and fail to realize that the ideal coach blends the two styles. There will be situations that require the coach to be highly directive in style (for example, explaining health and safety issues, starting the practice session), and others where the coach can involve the players in the decision making (for example, allowing them to chose a topic for a coaching session, agreeing on some group rules that would benefit the group). The flexibility in approach develops with experience.

What style do you adopt when coaching young players?

Coaches sometimes need to adapt their coaching style when working with different groups (young players, players with disabilities, adult players and so on) and in different environments. Remember that ability and reasons for participation vary across groups. Football clubs also exist at different levels in the game. A local kids' football club is very different to a professional football club. One may exist to provide opportunities to play and enjoy football, while the other may exist to play in the Premier League and in European competitions. The media focus on the professional game, and so it is important for coaches to appreciate the differences between junior players and professional players. They may wear the same make of football boots, have similar hairstyles and be competitive, but there are major differences. Coaches must recognize the different stages of psychological, physical and social development. Coaches must also understand why young people participate in football (see Chapters 1 and 2). Furthermore, children have a particular preference for the type of leadership they enjoy. Once you understand these issues, this can help to shape your leadership and coaching behaviour.

Best Practice Good leaders take into account the needs of the players, their stage of development, the players' preferred leadership style and the philosophy/type of club they are working at.

What type of coaches do children like? (Sports Coach UK, 2003, *The Successful Coach*)

Children like coaches who:

- Are friendly, patient, happy, understanding and have a sense of humour.
- Have credibility in the sport.
- Are firm but fair.
- Provide encouragement when it is due.
- Help to develop their skills.
- Are well organized.
- Take an interest in them.

Children do not like coaches who:

- Shout.
- Appear indecisive.

- Constantly say 'Well done', irrespective of the effort or skill demonstrated.

Wein, (2001) outlined some other coaching characteristics that can help a coach become well-accepted by their young players. These are:

- Good organization of training sessions, game arrangements and travel.
- Punctuality – starting and finishing on time.
- Dressing appropriately (professional appearance).
- Good communication skills – knowing how to explain concepts, how to listen and always having time for players.
- Emotionally stable – exercising self-control, transmitting calmness in the heat of competition and in the coaching environment. Do not lose composure with players, officials, parents and other team managers.
- Demonstrating true interest in the players (on and off the pitch).

Best Practice When you coach young players, make sure that your style suits their needs and preferences.

■ From Table 8, identify three things that you would like to improve on in the next month. Set some leadership behavioural goals for each month, rate yourself and compare your leadership scores. This will give you a profile of your leadership skills over the season. Look for patterns of progress but make sure that you keep doing the things that you are already good at. Build on your existing strengths and keep the good 'good'!

What is a coaching philosophy?

Top coaches and leaders have a coaching philosophy for their sport. This is a set of guidelines that governs their actions and behaviour (Sports Coach UK, 2003). It is based on the coach's beliefs and covers issues such as:

• The role of the coach in relation to others, e.g. players, parents.

• The relative importance of the outcome/result of the game in relation to the long-term development and well-being of the player.

• The importance of keeping to the rules and the meaning of fair play.

• The appropriate intensity of training and games for young players.

• The role of players in determining their own goals and the extent to which they should be responsible for their own behaviour and development.

Table 8 **A self tester for leadership qualities**

Rate yourself on these key characteristics that children like in a coaching situation. 1 = never and 5 = always.

		Never			Always	
1	I am friendly and have a sense of humour	1	2	3	4	5
2	I am patient, happy and understanding	1	2	3	4	5
3	I am firm but fair	1	2	3	4	5
4	I provide encouragement when it is due	1	2	3	4	5
5	I help develop their skills	1	2	3	4	5
6	I show good levels of organization in training sessions, game arrangements and travel	1	2	3	4	5
7	I am punctual – I start and finish on time	1	2	3	4	5
8	I am dressed appropriately (professional appearance)	1	2	3	4	5
9	I know how to explain concepts, how to listen and I always have time for players	1	2	3	4	5
10	I keep my composure with players, officials, parents and other team managers	1	2	3	4	5
11	I demonstrate true interest in the players (on and off the pitch); I am concerned for the player and the person	1	2	3	4	5

Key behaviours and strengths that I always show in my leadership:

1 _____

2 _____

3 _____

Key behaviours that I can improve upon during the next month:

1 _____

2 _____

3 _____

Best Practice A useful acronym for leadership is as follows:

Lead by example while being consistent with your philosophy.

Encourage others towards individual, team and club goals.

Athletes come first. Develop a player-centred philosophy.

Delegate – share responsibility and work with others.

Enthusiasm – share your passion and love of the game. Instill it in others.

Role model – be the best possible role model. 'Act as I do'.

Self-control – be in control of your emotions in competition and training environments.

Have and accept responsibility to your players and their families, your club and your sport.

Inclusive – keep everyone involved, all of the squad, parents, and your club.

Positive approach when dealing with players, parents, officials and other coaches.

What are the benefits of having a philosophy?

- It provides you with a personal and ethical framework within which you can work.

- It will remove uncertainty about discipline, training rules, code of conduct, and other facets of coaching (Martens, 1987).

- Having a philosophy and working within its framework leads to a consistent approach in your coaching. Players like coaches who are consistent in their coaching. (Taken from Sports Coach UK (2003) *The Successful Coach*.)

■ Consider your own coaching philosophy. Think about why you are currently coaching or want to coach. List ways in which your coaching philosophy influences the way you work as a coach. Consider how important it is for the coach, players, parents and club to have a similar philosophy.

Quote | 'Praise your players. Inspire and motivate your players with praise. Ten years from now it won't matter what your record was. Will your kids love you or hate you?'

Best Practice To be an effective coach it is important to understand your own coaching philosophy.

Develop a player-centred approach

A basic principle of using sport psychology with players is to be aware, as a coach or manager that the player is the key to everything. The player should be the focal point of your attention (see Chapter 1). Develop an attitude that it is your responsibility, as an adult coach, to continue to improve your own skills and knowledge to enable you to better understand and support your players. Be there for the player's benefit.

Best Practice Develop a player-centred philosophy. Constantly try to improve your own knowledge for the players' benefit.

Quote | 'Attitude is contagious. Is your attitude to coaching and leadership worth catching?'

Summary

- Leadership is essentially an individual acting to influence others towards set goals.

- There is no definitive list of qualities but there are some that many successful coaches have in common. Coaches can develop these qualities.

- Coaches often think that they have to be one or the other of the two main leadership styles (autocratic or democratic), and fail to realize that the ideal coach blends the two styles together.

- Good leaders take into account the needs of the players, their stage of development, the players' preferred leadership style, and the philosophy/type of club they are working at.

- When you coach young players, make sure your style suits their needs and preferences.

- To be an effective coach it is important to understand your own coaching philosophy. Once you identify it, then be consistent in your approach.

- Develop a player-centred philosophy.

- For the players' benefit, constantly try to improve your own knowledge.

- Good leaders are open to new ideas and are able to take on board other views.

Self testers

1 What is leadership?

2 Name five qualities of an effective leader.

3 What type of coach do players like?

Action plan

Philosophy target Over the next month, develop your own philosophy by determining your views on some key issues. Make sure you share them with players, parents, family, other coaches and your club. By discussing them with other coaches you begin to develop a greater awareness of the coaching process. You may even want to encourage the club to develop a club philosophy that all coaches, parents and players refer to. Your philosophy may change over time, but it is important that you make a start.

Chapter 6

LEARNING

Communication

THIS CHAPTER WILL:
- Describe the process of communication.
- Explain the importance of both verbal and non-verbal communication.
- Help you increase your effectiveness when communicating with your players.
- Suggest ways to help you to develop better working relationships with your players.
- Explore how you can create a better football environment for your players by the effective use of communication.
- Help you prepare to get the best out of your players.

Quote | 'Coaching is an act of communication – of explaining what you want of people in a way that allows them to do it.'
Bill Parcells, US National Football League Coach (cited in Beswick, 2001)

Coaching is described in Chapter 5 as a people business. Effective coaching is not just about developing skills and improving performance; it is about building good relationships with players, parents, other coaches and officials. The skill of good communication is a key component of successful coaching (Sports Coach UK, 2003). To become an excellent leader/coach you must develop the communication skills to move people into action. Coaches instruct, encourage, discipline, organize and evaluate players' performances, all of which require sending messages (Martens, 1987). Coaches must be able to interact with a variety of people in a range of situations and styles. The situations vary from coaching sessions, team talks and meetings with parents and league officials, while the styles vary from casual and informal to formal.

A broader understanding of communication

Communication is a two-way process – one of giving and receiving information. It has many aspects such as talking, listening, pleading,

arguing, negotiating, encouraging, consoling, both verbal and non-verbal. It is often assumed that giving information is more important, but this is rarely the case. Coaches need to understand their players, and to do this they have to listen to them and ask questions.

Verbal communication

Verbal communication involves conveying messages that have both content (i.e. what is said) and form (i.e. how it is sent). Many coaches are very good at giving information that is high in content, for instance, when introducing new tactics or technical skills. However, players may 'switch off', become bored, confused and even frustrated if too much information is given. Furthermore, when coaches continually use verbal instruction, they become the main actors in the coaching theatre thereby limiting or stopping the active participation of the players (Wein, 2001). However, by involving the players through asking questions and listening to them, a coach obliges them to think, collect information, evaluate and judge, and create and invent. This involves and encourages players to take more responsibility for their own learning and development.

Best Practice Too much verbal instruction from coaches limits the participation and enjoyment of players. Involve them through asking questions and listening to them.

Non-verbal communication

Non-verbal communications are the messages we send to people without uttering a word – 'It's not what you say, but how you say it'. Research from Albert Mehrabian, 1968 (cited in Sports Coach UK (2003) Chapter 5) on communication between two people has shown that the relative impact of the message is as follows: words contribute to just 7 per cent, the way the words are spoken contribute 38 per cent and non-verbal information (e.g. gestures, expressions) contribute 55 per cent. This research suggests that over 90 per cent of information is conveyed non-verbally. Consequently coaches should recognize the impact of non-verbal information they send (often unconsciously) through gestures, bodily posture etc. (Sports Coach UK, 2003).

Paralanguage

This refers to all the vocal components of speech, considered separately from the actual meaning of their words. Often the way information is conveyed (pitch, rhythm, speed, loudness) can hold greater meaning for performers than the actual content of the words.

Coaches often say, 'A picture paints a thousand words'. What type of picture are we presenting with our non-verbal behaviour?

Gestures

Gestures and various body movements also have particular meaning. Contrast the coach who stands or sits with his arms folded with the coach who shakes hands with a player or gives them a thumbs-up gesture in a game. The latter is a positive message while the former may show a lack of interest in events or a lack of openness.

Posture

We communicate with our posture and the way we walk. An erect posture with a purposeful walk displays feelings of openness, confidence and energy. This is important in the football environment because it will influence how other people interact with the coach. Players recognize when coaches are not feeling their best and may not fully co-operate with the coach during a training session. If the coach displays confidence and enthusiasm, this is a far better starting point for a coaching session or team talk.

Touching

In football the coach could use touching to calm a player (for instance, a hand on the shoulder), to express satisfaction with players' performance (a handshake, a pat on the back) or to interrupt a conversation (a light touch on the arm), depending on the context.

Facial expressions

The face is a powerful source of expression. The eyes and mouth communicate a great deal. Coaches communicate a variety of messages from dissatisfaction and frustration through to interest in what is being said. The amount of time that we spend in eye contact with someone is another way in which we communicate. Coaches need to show an interest in what their players say and, likewise, maintain eye contact when they have some criticism to give to a player.

Personal space

People communicate by the way they use space – the distance between the speaker and the recipients. This can also include how a meeting is planned with furniture, seating arrangements and so on. Coaches need to be aware of this when communicating with individual players and groups. Respect individuals' personal space and avoid rows of seats when conducting meetings with players. A circular or horseshoe arrangement of chairs is less threatening and more inclusive.

Quote | 'Your ability to communicate with your players will determine your success.'

Observation of players

The players' non-verbal language will also give the coach information regarding the effectiveness of his or her own verbal and non-verbal language. The coach will gain some indication of their interest levels, attention and understanding.

Congruence

It is important in coaching that there is congruence (a match) between what is being said verbally and what is being expressed non-verbally. To illustrate, the coach says they are happy with the players' performance and this is reflected in their body language (open body language, facial language) and tone of voice. This match is important, otherwise players and parents may get mixed messages from coaches.

Listening – receiving messages effectively

Listening is an important aspect of communication. Many coaches love talking, being in charge and organizing, but they are often poor listeners. Players want to know that their coach listens to them, and they want to feel satisfied that they have been heard and understood. Coaches who are good listeners do not miss out on information that could be of importance to them. It could be information from a player, parent or another coach. Good listening is hard work. It requires intense concentration. Active listening involves paraphrasing what you think the person said, for example, 'Let me see if I've got this right, you said. . .', 'What you are telling me is . . .'. It can also include asking questions for clarification or to get more background information.

Besides active listening, the following will improve your listening skills (Martens, 1987):

- Be mentally prepared to listen.
- Listen to the content of the message. Forget the appearance or reputation of the speaker.
- Listen with your eyes. Observe the body language of the speaker.
- Listen with empathy. Great leaders have the ability to adopt the perspective of the other person, understanding how that person perceives events and experiences emotions. This is not

to be confused with sympathy. A sympathetic person feels emotions of regret for a person experiencing trouble.

- Listen with openness. You cannot hear a message if you are evaluating or judging it while it is being delivered.

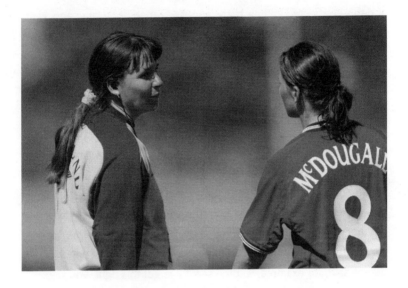

Best Practice Players who feel responsible and aware of their own performance tend to improve at a faster rate. To encourage these two qualities, coaches can simply ask effective questions.

How players learn

Players learn in a number of different ways and have preferred learning styles. Essentially, players learn best from the following sources of information, but this will vary between players:

- Visual – through pictures and images.
- Sound – through sounds and the spoken word.
- Senses – through feelings and physical interaction.

It is important as a coach that you consider all learning styles and deliver sessions that develop players by appealing to a wide range of learning styles. For example, you can show players what you are about to do in training on a tactics board (visual), you can describe and explain to them (sound), and you can ask them to demonstrate (senses).

▨   Think of some ways that you could incorporate this principle about learning styles into your training environment. What are the benefits for your players? Do you organize sessions based around your own preferred learning style or the group in general? When you next wish to introduce a new idea to the team or to an individual player, plan how you can offer the idea in the three ways described above, i.e. using visual aids, using sound, and by asking players to practise, even without a ball, in order to feel the sensation of a new skill or strategy.

You can implement the learning-style requirements in your coaching environment by:

- Drawing diagrams of the specific session, backing this up with words, and displaying the diagrams in the dressing room. You might also show a coaching video or clip from a match that shows what the players are going to practise (visual).
- Explaining (verbal) the diagrams to the group.
- Putting some questions up on the dressing room wall and asking the players to show you the answers on a tactics board (visual).
- Doing the work on the pitch (senses).
- Asking the players to reflect on the session and to write down or draw what they have learned and how they feel about their work.

Best Practice Use a variety of teaching methods, styles and aids to help all players to learn in their preferred style.

▓ Over the next month, see how many of the above tips you can integrate into your delivery of coaching sessions or that you can use on match day. Remember to keep it simple!

Demonstrations – 'A picture paints a thousand words'

Demonstrations play an important part in the learning process. They provide opportunities for players to model skilled behaviour. They also provide a visual image for learning. Coaches should ensure that the demonstration is reasonably correct from a technical perspective. The coach can demonstrate to the group or use one of the players to demonstrate. When you set up a demonstration ensure that:

- You have gained the players' attention. You should have their eye contact and wait until they have stopped talking, moving the ball, etc.
- The group is positioned so that they can all see you.
- The demonstration is repeated a number of times so that everyone understands what is required.
- The demonstration is silent (no verbal instructions), for players can only focus on one aspect while learning. Before or after the demonstration you can add some verbal instructions.
- The player's attention is directed to a few crucial messages. Avoid overloading them with information.
- You avoid jargon and other technical terms. Keep it simple and concise.

- Demonstrations are at the appropriate level for the players, i.e. they match their ability and stage of development.

- Remember to use people's names. This puts people at ease and is courteous (Beswick, 2001).

Feedback: Bite-sized digestible building blocks for improvement

Feedback is essential for players to improve their performance. Through feedback, coaches should aim to give praise, build upon existing strengths and improve weaknesses. Feedback helps the players reduce the number of errors made. In football, feedback is mainly based on the coaches' observations (visual). Some coaches also use video or match analysis (systematic pen and paper observations) to provide feedback to players. Players can also get internal feedback from their own senses when they perform a technique. They can feel the movement, see the outcome (ball hits target) and hear the sound of the action (hear the sound of the ball being struck). Coaches can draw the players' attention to this source of feedback. When providing feedback –

- Give players time to consider their own feedback before providing any additional external feedback.

- Keep it positive. Players respond better to praise.

- Young players need to be acknowledged. They get highly motivated if they receive praise when they are trying to master a new skill. Through praise they are encouraged to try harder. To children under 12, the coach and parent are like a mirror in which they see their capacity or incapacity (Wein, 2001). That is why coaches need to be positive, to praise the child frequently, and keep critical comments to a minimum.

- Take care not to overuse praise such as 'Well done'. If you use it too often, it loses its effect. Balance its use with more technical information, e.g. 'Well done, good pass. You kept the ball low', 'Good pass, you hit the bottom half of the ball'.

- Coaches should also be able to accept feedback from other coaches and adults regarding their coaching performance. They should encourage feedback from their players. This is not to be confused with 'fishing for compliments'. Coaches could get the players to fill in a small, anonymous questionnaire. This approach is likely to get more input from young players.

Statistic

England's most successful manager is Sir Alf Ramsay. The highlight of his 11-year career was managing England to World Cup glory in 1966. His record as manager was: his team played 113, won 69, drew 27 and lost 17.

• 'Know when to put the ball away'. Coaches need to know when to switch off and stop providing feedback to the player. There comes a time after the session or game where it is best to move on and think about other things. Likewise, players do not like to be constantly reminded of their mistakes.

Giving feedback – the sandwich technique

Coaches are always striving to be positive towards players when giving feedback however, there are times when criticism is necessary. Unfortunately players become defensive when they are criticized and they fail to take on board the information. The 'sandwich approach' has been identified as an effective way to give constructive feedback in a sensitive yet effective manner. This feedback technique involves three sequential elements (Weinberg and Gould, 2003):

1   A positive statement, e.g. 'Good effort'.

2   Future-orientated instructions, e.g. 'Next time, make sure you hit the ball with your laces'.

3   A compliment. This builds trust and rapport.

The complete 'sandwich' could be or in this case, would be: 'Good effort. Next time, make sure you hit the ball with your laces. Keep up the good work.'

It is important that coaches do not provide too much feedback as this can interfere with a player's enjoyment of the session or it can overload the player with too much information.

Best Practice   Keep looking for opportunities to provide positive feedback. Players respond better to praise. Make your feedback specific, e.g. 'great early pass' rather than 'well played'.

TheFA

LEARNING

Summary

- Good coaching is as much about how you 'say' as what you 'say'.

- Communication is a two-way process – one of giving and receiving information.

- Good communication leads to more effective coaching and working relationships with players.

- Know when to stop providing feedback!

Self testers

1 Explain and describe the sandwich technique of feedback.

2 Name three ways players learn to receive information.

3 How much information is received by players from non-verbal means?

Action plan

Over the next two months, get another coach to evaluate you on the principles described in this chapter: how often do you give informational feedback? How often do you give positive feedback? Do you use the sandwich technique and do you listen to your players? Does this match your own evaluation?

If you do not want to have such an evaluation then get a friend to video your coaching session so you can evaluate your own performance without any outside input.

Draw up some targets from this chapter or from the observations of your coaching session to help improve your communication skills. Be patient and remember that you can improve with a systematic approach.

Chapter 7

LEARNING

Goal-setting

THIS CHAPTER WILL:
- Describe what goal-setting is.
- Help you to understand the principles of goal-setting.
- Explain how to create SMART and SMARTER goals.
- Describe the difference between outcome, performance and process goals.
- Explore common problems in goal-setting.
- Explain 'doing' goal-setting.

Quote | 'Goals are the "building blocks" of improvement.'

What are goals?

A goal is an aim or target that someone is trying to achieve. It is a standard of attainment.

Why are goals useful?

Goals improve the quality of your effort, that is to say, they can help improve the *purpose* and *quality* of training because they direct attention to the task. Goals encourage people to work *SMART* as well as *hard*. They also increase effort and persistence by providing feedback in relation to the player's own performance. In this way, goals can maintain motivation on a day-to-day basis as well as over time. They also increase the intensity of the effort required to satisfy whatever the reason is that young players play football. In other words, goals enhance motivation. The final way in which goals can affect performance is through the development of relevant learning strategies. For example, if a player's goal is to increase his or her percentage of effective crosses made from 45 per cent to 70 per cent then he or she may develop ways to achieve that in body balance, striking technique and the curve put on the ball.

The ability to be a rubber-ball competitor, that is, to be able to bounce back from performance set-backs as a result of increased determination to succeed, is seen as important in studies of 'mental toughness' in sports performers. The role of goals in increased determination to succeed and more performer persistence is echoed in the following quotation.

Quote | 'If you haven't set yourself meaningful goals, it's all too easy to turn back and go home when it's a miserable day and training doesn't appeal. Goal-setting is the key to motivation.' Kirsten Barnes, Canadian rower and double Olympic gold medallist

Principles of goal-setting: SMART goals

A common formula for developing effective goals is the SMART system, which recommends goals that are **S**pecific, **M**easurable, **A**ction-oriented, **R**ealistic and **T**imed.

- **S**pecific: This refers to the detailed description of the desired behaviour (i.e. the actual behaviour you wish to achieve, or level of mastery you wish to attain); so do not be vague! Specific goals tend to result in higher levels of performance than no goals or 'Do your best' goals. 'Go out and do your best' goals, contrary to common belief, are not as effective in enhancing motivation and performance as encouraging players to go out on the pitch and try and achieve a specific goal (task).

- **M**easurable: Effective goals are measurable. Higher motivation is gained when you have a way to measure the progress you are making towards achieving your goal. You will need to establish a 'starting-point' measurement, and from there players can see and monitor their improvement, resulting in increased confidence – in other words, give the goal a measure or a number.

- **A**ction-orientated: The goal should be written in a way which provides information on *how* to get to the goal. For example, 'I will practise my free kicks every other day for 20 minutes', rather than, 'I will increase the percentage of free kicks I get on target from 50 per cent to 70 per cent'.

- **Realistic:** Goals must be challenging yet attainable. They should be attainable if the player works really hard to achieve them. Be careful of setting goals that a player has little chance of achieving and that result in failure and a loss of confidence, and possibly motivation. Goals that are too easy are equally as ineffective because they make the player think that successes can be achieved with less than maximum effort. Moreover, be flexible: different players in the same squad should be set personal goals in addition to group goals – not one general goal.

- **Timed:** Goals should be timed. Quite simply, you need to know by when you want to achieve your goal. Goals should be given a 'due in by' date which is written in the goal statement. This is a reasonably timed date in the future when the goal is to be achieved by.

▨ Develop a SMART goal for your team. Ensure the goal includes each aspect described above.

Principles of goal-setting: SMARTER goals

Two additional principles appear in some other goal-setting systems. These are **E**lasticity and **R**epeatable to turn the word 'SMART' into 'SMARTER'.

- **Elasticity:** This refers to having a 'window' target as opposed to a single-point target. A player setting a goal to score between 18 and 23 goals during the season rather than 20 goals is an example of a 'window' goal. Window targets are seen as effective because they are more flexible and more likely to be seen as achievable by the player. They are also less prone to result in a self-limiting mind-set if the player and/or team is performing very well.

- **Repeatability:** This requires the player or team to meet the goal more than once so that the goal is less likely to be attributed to luck or coincidence, but rather to effort, ability and performance improvement. An alternative meaning for the 'R' is 'Recorded' as there is a suggestion that there is more 'stickability' to goals once they are written down. This is where the phrase 'Ink it, don't think it!' comes from.

Principles of goal-setting: SMARTS goals

Another goal-setting acronym is SMARTS. The additional 'S' stands for Self-determined. It is important that the player has as much involvement and control in the setting of the goal as possible. It is crucial that the person feels as though the goals belong to them and that the goals are not controlling them (see Chapter 2).

Types of goals

There are three types of goals:

- Outcome goals.
- Performance goals.
- Process goals.

Outcome goals

Outcome goals are essentially *winning and losing* goals. This goal is often not in a player's control because achieving this type of goal depends, at least in part, on the ability and play of the opposition. For example, a team may set a goal to 'win the match', then play really well but lose and not achieve their goal. These goals are often misleading and do not tell the true story. For instance, in the situation just described, the team could play really poorly and win. In so doing they achieve the goal, but probably only because the opposition played even worse. In this case, where does the improvement in performance come from?

Performance goals

Performance goals are 'How am I doing compared to myself?' goals. They are based upon the player's actual performance in relation to their own standard of excellence (for example, increasing the number of crosses put in from three to six). Performance goals are targets which are in relation to the player's own personal ability. These targets basically say that the competition is against yourself. This may sound a little strange, but in essence this translates to, 'Can I do better today than I did yesterday?'

■　Ask players to set themselves a performance goal in their next training session or match. An example for a wide player could be to deliver three quality crosses into the box. An example for a defender could be to make three quality long-range passes into the centre forwards.

Process goals

Process goals are the 'How to do' goals of the goal-setting world. They focus the player's attention on specific tasks because their focus is on the specific mechanisms and behaviours of how to perform the skill (for instance, knee over the ball and so on).

■   When working on a particular skill in your next session, ask players to identify a key element of that skill (for example, keep the knee over the ball when striking a low drive). This 'process' goal can be 'imaged' (see Chapter 8) before and during the actual practice.

Best Practice Football players should use all three types of goals, with specific emphasis on performance and process goals because they are under one's control.

Short-, medium- and long-term goals

It can be beneficial to view short-, medium-, and long-term goals as a staircase. Players should use all of these types of goals. Long-term goals provide direction and purpose, whereas short-term goals provide day-to-day motivation. Short-term goals make the long-term goals seem less daunting and thus more achievable by breaking them down into more do-able pieces. Short-term goals are the 'building blocks' of improvement.

■   From the list of goals below, decide which is outcome, which is performance and which is process:

• To win this match.
• To make sure you keep your eye on the ball as you strike it for a cross, at the same time saying to yourself 'eyes down.'
• To put in six crosses in a game.

Common problems in goal-setting

- Failing to set specific goals.
- Setting too many goals – this is a common problem and one which leads to none of the goals really being strived for.
- Failing to adjust goals – often because the goals are not committed to in the first place. But also because the task of monitoring all the goals is too difficult and unrealistic a goal in itself!
- Failing to set performance and process goals – the coach, in conjunction with the player, could set process goals for each player at the start of the session. These could then be written down and referred to throughout the session.
- Insufficient monitoring and evaluation – coaches and parents should refer players to their goals more regularly and frequently. To do this, it is best during the very first goal-setting meeting to commit several dates to review the progress of the goals.
- Insufficient player involvement in the process – this is very often the cause of poor commitment to the goals. Players need to be involved in all aspects of the goal-setting process. Players, depending on their maturity, can be actively involved to varying

degrees in the process, to the extent of actually designing and completing the paperwork themselves. After all, whose goals are they?

- There is often very little acknowledgement of either the success or failure of the goals, i.e. positive or negative reinforcement.

- Inadequate support for the goals from others such as parents, other family members and coach. This lack of support from a 'significant other' invariably happens if that person has not been involved in the goal-setting process in the first place.

▓▓ Look at the following goals and place on a scale from 1–10 how specific they are with 1 being not specific at all and 10 being very specific.

1 To be the best player I can be. **/10**

2 To improve my defending. **/10**

3 To increase the accuracy of my shooting from outside the box. **/10**

4 To call for the ball and risk to make things happen when losing by a goal or drawing with less than ten minutes left. **/10**

5 To increase my successful right-foot crossing on the run from 50 per cent to 70 per cent. **/10**

Doing goal-setting

We have looked at what goals are, and now we can explore the practical part of effective goal-setting – how you go about doing it.

1 Either the coach and player have a meeting, or the coach, player and parents, as appropriate. Strengths and weaknesses (or better still 'areas of improvement') are assessed, and some common ground is established. To get the conversation flowing, it is often helpful to ask the player to work through a performance profile with the coach, detailing areas of strengths and weaknesses.

Good questions to ask:

- 'What are some of the things you would like to achieve in football?'
- 'What do you want to achieve long term?'
- 'What does success look like?'
- 'What are the positive benefits of achieving your goals?'
- 'What are the consequences of not achieving your goals?'
- 'How do you think you might go about achieving them?'
- 'What do you think you will want and need to do in order to achieve them?'

2 The coach and player write 'goal-test' dates in the diary, and arrange a time for a meeting on that date when the goal will be evaluated either on the pitch or simply in a meeting, depending upon the type of goal being tested.

Good questions to ask:

- 'When do you think it may be possible to achieve each goal by?'
- 'When do you want to achieve it by?'
- 'How will you measure it?'
- 'How will you know when you have achieved it?'
- 'How do you feel about achieving the goal?'

3 The goals for the player should be written down. To help the player to see the relationship between their short-term and longer-term goals, present them in a picture format. For example, as a staircase, a ladder, a rock climber climbing up a sheer face or a football cup draw moving from quarter-finals to the final. The more presentable the goals are to the player, the more likely they are to refer to them.

4 Suggest to the player that they place their goal sheet somewhere where it will be seen on a daily basis, e.g. the fridge, bedroom door, toilet door, back of front car seat. Ask the question, 'What support do you need to achieve your goals and from whom?' The coach could also ask, 'What could I do to support you?'

5   Elicit player responsibility for the goal by asking the question, 'How much personal control or influence do you think you have over your goal?' and 'Who is responsible for achieving this goal?'

6   Gain acknowledgement of the level of importance. To encourage the player to talk about how important achieving the goal is to them, the coach could simply ask the question, 'On a scale of 1 to 10 with 10 being really important, how important is it to you to achieve this goal?'

7   Gain commitment from the player by asking, 'On a scale of 1 to 10, how confident are you that you will stick to trying to achieve your goals?' and 'What do you think you can guarantee?'

8   Goal progress should be evaluated in a monthly group session with all players and coaches present (these dates should be included on your annual planner). Players can talk about their own rate of progress for their goals, and other players can comment. Players should bring evidence of the degree of their progress.

Summary

- **Goals are the building blocks of improvement.**

- **Goals improve the quality of effort.**

- **Goals encourage more focus and intensity in training and competition.**

- **Use SMART, SMARTER and SMARTS goal models.**

- **Encourage players to use performance and process goals in training and competition.**

- **Use long-, medium- and short-term goals.**

- **'Ink it!' Don't 'think it!'**

Self testers

1   What use are goals to your players?

2   How can goal-setting help focus players on performing to their potential?

3   Name and describe a model of goal-setting.

Action plan

Get smart   Over the next month, develop a goal-setting sheet for your players, and organize a meeting to explain to your players the benefits of goal-setting and how to use SMARTER goals. Ask them to set their own long-term (one year), and short-term (one week) goals. Review these regularly with your players and monitor the improvements made.

Chapter 8

Imagery

> THIS CHAPTER WILL:
> - Help you to understand what imagery is.
> - Explain how imagery works.
> - Describe the different types of imagery.
> - Explore the different uses of imagery.
> - Explain when to use imagery.
> - Suggest ways in which imagery can help a player's confidence, control and composure.

Sportspeople and leaders often speak about seeing success before it happens. Think like a winner, speak like a winner, act like a winner, and you have a great chance of becoming a winner.

> David Beckham places the ball on the grass. The white of the ball stands out against the lush green surface. The dew on the grass has made the ball a little slippery and damp. He spins the ball around so the red logo faces exactly where he wants to strike it. He stands up. He feels the breeze against his face. He looks at the keeper. Bright yellow shirt looks small against the massive

goal. He sees the back of the net blowing in the wind. Shortly, the ball will hit the back of the net. He glances at the ref, all in black, he raises his whistle and you hear the shrill. He starts his run up and strikes the ball so it spins around the wall. It glides over the keeper into the back of the net. 1–0.

Reading through the above passage as a football player, it is difficult not to think of the process and thrill of a free kick flying into the back of the net. This is imagery or visualization. When your players look at videos or programmes of their favourite players and then remember things from them later on, they are using imagery.

Of the many routines available to increase mental strength, imagery is an easily used skill; particularly if you bear in mind that most people use their imagination and day dream often. Imagery is an extremely portable

skill that can be utilized any time and in any place (for example, when waiting in queues, travelling to and from games and in the time prior to matches), and it is an ideal technique to use at night just before going to sleep. Like physical skills, imagery skills must be practised and learned to be most useful.

'Imagery', 'visualization', 'mental practice' and 'mental rehearsal' are all common terms used to describe the process of using your imagination to see yourself performing, practising a sport-related skill or competing in a certain situation. Through regular imaging you can train both your mind and body to perform consistently during training and high-pressure situations.

What is imagery?

- Using your imagination to see yourself performing or practising a sport-related skill or imagining yourself competing in a certain situation.
- Creating in our minds the information normally detected by our sense organs, i.e. recreating pictures, recalling sounds and tastes, recapturing a feeling of movement and reliving emotions, almost as if they were really happening.

Imagery is a form of simulation. It is a method of using all the senses to create or recreate an experience in the mind. Athletes refer to imagery as 'Going to the movies in your mind'. It is a powerful and underused tool, and it can help players in a number of ways. Studies have shown that 90 per cent of Olympic athletes use imagery regularly and as an integral part of their training programme (Orlick and Partington, 1988, see Table 9). It is similar to a real experience, but it occurs in the mind.

Table 9 **Example of Olympic athletes' use of imagery**

Performer interviews

A highly successful Olympian pistol shooter stated:

> 'As for success imagery, I would imagine myself, "How would a champion act? How would a champion feel? How would she perform on the line?" This helped me find out about myself, what worked and didn't work for me. Then, as the actual roles I had imagined came along, and I achieved them, that in turn helped me believe that I would be the Olympic champion.'

A highly successful Olympic swimmer stated:

> 'I started visualising in 1978. My visualisation has been refined more and more as the years go on. That is really what got me the world record and the Olympic medals. I see myself swimming the race before the race really happens, and I try to be on the splits. I concentrate on attaining the splits I have set out to do. About 15 minutes before the race I always visualise the race in my mind and "see" how it will go . . . You are really swimming the race. You are visualising it from behind the block. In my mind, I go up and down the pool, rehearsing all parts of the race, visualising how I actually feel in the water.'

A highly successful Olympic springboard diver stated:

> 'I did my dives in my head all the time. At night, before going to sleep, I always did my dives. Ten dives. I started with a front dive, the first one I had to do at the Olympics, and I did everything as if I was actually there. I saw myself on the board with the same bathing suit. Everything was the same. I saw myself in the pool at the Olympics doing my dives. If the dive was wrong, I went back and started over again. It takes a good hour to do perfect imagery of all my dives, but for me it was better than a workout. Sometimes I would take the weekend off and do imagery five times a day. I felt like I was on the board and I did each dive so many times in my mind.

> 'It took me a long time to control my images and perfect my imagery, maybe a year, doing it every day. At first I couldn't see

myself, I always saw someone else, or I would see my dives wrong all the time. I would get an image of hurting myself, or tripping on the board, or I would "see" something done really bad. As I continued to work on it, I got to the point where I could see myself doing the perfect dive and the crowd yelling at the Olympics. But it took me a long time. I read everything I had to do and I knew my dive by heart. Then I started to see myself on the board doing my perfect dive. But some days I couldn't see it, or it was a bad dive in my head. I worked at it so much it got to the point that I could do all my dives easily.'

A highly successful Olympian figure skater stated:

'My imagery is more just feel. I don't think it's visual at all. When I'm watching it on video I look visually at it and then I get this internal feeling. When I'm actually doing it I get the same feeling inside. It is a very internal feeling that is hard to explain. You have to experience it, and once you do, then you know what you are going after. I can even get a feeling for an entire program. Sometimes in a practice I get myself psyched into a program that will win the Olympics, like I won the long program last year. I step on the ice and go to my starting position and I get this feeling, "I'm at the Olympic games", and I sort of get the whole program flashed before my eyes and I get this internal feeling of how this program will be, and usually I'm fresh and usually it will be the perfect program. I don't just step out there in training and say, here we go, another program.'

Source: Orlick and Partington, 1988

Studies show that imagery of a successful performance outcome produces better performance than imagery of an unsuccessful outcome. So, if you think and see yourself performing well, you will generally perform well.

Statistic

The record for England's most prolific penalty scorer is shared by Alan Shearer and Ron Flowers (a player from the 1960's) with six penalties each.

Thus, imagery is what happens when we experience an event without actually being there. It is an experience similar to a sensory experience (seeing, hearing, feeling), but it occurs without the usual external experience; it is like playing a video in your mind. This video could recall something you actually did in the past (scoring a good goal) or something you want to do (score a good goal!). It could also watch someone else perform, for example, Michael Owen outrunning the Argentina back-line to score a wonder goal. The experience is basically a memory recall or an imagined event. Young players have a tremendous imagination and are great at painting these pictures in their mind's eye. The skill appears to reduce as children grow, but should be developed as any other skill in the game. All players use imagery, but for most it is not structured.

The amazing thing with imagery is that the mind does not distinguish between the real thing and the imagined thing. Therefore, if you see yourself performing a skill, the mind cannot tell if this actually happened. This is a great tool for any player because imagery can be a form of training. Incredible really.

How imagery works

There are numerous theories on how imagery works. Since your mind controls your body, it is sensible to assume that the mind–body connection is an important and essential relationship. This connection occurs whether you actually execute a task or just think about executing one. One of the most famous imagery experiments involved wiring electrodes to the legs of an alpine skier to test out the notion that vivid imagery produces electrical activity within the muscles similar to the electrical impulses produced during actual movement. The experiment clearly showed that when the skier was sitting down, simply thinking of skiing downhill, similar electrical patterns were found in the muscles as if he had actually been skiing!

By imaging or visualizing yourself playing football, the muscles you would use to physically perform the task are stimulated at a very low level. This gentle muscle activation is not strong enough to produce the actual movements you are imaging, but the stimulation does serve to establish a blueprint for that particular movement or situation. By recreating the appropriate sensory information that contributes to the successful execution of a skill or the correct behaviour for a specific situation, you will strengthen the blueprint so that it becomes more likely that you are able to produce the correct response while under pressure. If you are serious about improving the standard of your performance, you will need to develop the skill of effectively imaging both the technical and tactical elements of football.

| Quote | 'Before a match whilst I am standing in the changing room, then whilst standing singing the National Anthem, I mentally rehearse flying out of the circle and making that interception! I image the movement, how it will feel and the emotion of the experience.' Amanda Newton, England National Netball Squad Vice Captain, 2000 |

What makes imagery effective?

Imagery is more when you make it realistic and as close to real life as possible. For an image to be effective, it must be vivid and controllable.

- **Vivid – this refers to the clarity and sharpness of the image. For example, the more you integrate each of your senses into your images, the greater the potential effects are for influencing your physical performance.**

- **Controllability – this refers to your ability to influence the content of the image. For example, the time taken to image an event should parallel the time it would take to physically complete the event.**

What will I see when I use imagery?

When you use imagery it is likely that you will see yourself performing either from an internal or an external perspective. You may use just one or both types of imagery. You may find that you alternate between the two imagery perspectives as you recreate a football scenario in your mind. The internal perspective is particularly suitable for the mental practice of specific skills. The external perspective is useful for imagery sessions that focus on tactical rehearsal or that review your performance. You should use whichever perspective you feel most comfortable with.

- **Internal perspective – as if you were looking through your own eyes. The internal perspective replicates exactly what you would see during a performance.**

- **External perspective – as you would see yourself if you were watching yourself on a video or on television.**

Best Practice Ask your players to use imagery from both internal and external perspectives. Players should use bright colourful pictures with sounds and feelings. If players find it difficult to imagine themselves in action, start by asking them to 'imagine' their favourite player executing the skill they wish to perform. Coaches can check on imaging ability by asking their player(s) to act out the skill (i.e. actually perform the skill without a ball) in slow motion, so that the coach can evaluate the execution.

There is no right or wrong type of imagery and players can easily flick from one type of image to another. Generally, the internal perspective is more 'real' because the player is actually feeling he or she is in the situation. Because of this, and since it is considered to be more related to the senses rather than only visual, it has been suggested to be initially favoured by players.

Players should be encouraged to try both types of imagery, and they will normally end up with a preference that suits them as individuals.

Imagery can also be used in real time or slow motion. Real-time imagery occurs when your thoughts coincide with the actual timing of the task, while slow motion can be used to help develop a particular skill or simply to see the outcome of a shot. For example, to image the free kick flying into the net is something Gianfranco Zola of Chelsea often spoke about.

| Quote | 'The success I have at free kicks is 5 per cent skill and 95 per cent successful imagery.' Gianfranco Zola |

■　Ask your players to imagine themselves carrying out a task (for instance, receiving and controlling the ball and then passing to a teammate) from both an internal and an external perspective. Ask them to use as many senses as possible in both cases. Which method did they prefer?

Why is imagery important?

While imagery is used for a number of reasons, the two main purposes seem to be to prime the player for peak performance (motivational imagery) and to enhance skill learning. Motivational imagery is used, for example, to set goals, control emotions and stress, and to gain and maintain self-confidence. Skill learning can include learning new skills, rehearsing game plans, strategies and routines. Football players tend to use imagery more for its motivational function than for its learning function.

> Imagery can be a highly motivating tool. Athletes instructed to imagine successfully performing a simple task voluntarily practised longer than others.

Table 10 **Benefits and uses of different types of imagery**

Perspective	Benefits
External	You can view yourself as if on video.
	You can see the whole picture from different angles (good for strategy purposes).
	You can spin yourself around and see actions from various positions.
	May be most useful when learning a new skill.
Internal	A more realistic viewpoint (seeing the picture as if you are in the action).
	A more realistic experience (particularly when using all senses).
	Can be used to effectively rehearse things you wish to do in a game.
Either perspective	Can be used in real time or slow motion.
	The player can zoom in or out of the picture.
	Can be used even if the player has never executed the task.

Self-confidence is the most consistent factor in distinguishing highly successful from less successful players. Given the relationship between self-confidence and sport performance, there is a need among players, coaches and sport psychologists to have strategies to enhance self-confidence. Mental imagery may be one such strategy.

If previous performance accomplishments are the major sources of self-confidence (see Chapter 3), players should develop a long-term memory bank containing all the good moments to replay at will. They should also be encouraged to use a selective short-term memory for things that were not so good – forget the missed shot or pass (after you've learned what went wrong!). The more frequently the good clips are replayed, the more confident the player becomes.

A second source of self-confidence is known as 'vicarious experience' or living through the experiences of others. The implication of this aspect of confidence is that when players see their role models do something, they will try to emulate them. Just as importantly, players can use their own teammates as role models, and by seeing them complete a skill, they can be motivated to do the same. Furthermore, as already mentioned, the recall of these images does not even have to be a recall from a real occurrence. It is an amazing skill to use.

Therefore, a key element in imagery is to imagine successful performances – either a rerun of previous successes or imagining the performance of a new task. Players should focus on the key factors that contribute to this success and develop strategies to enhance performance in similar situations in the future (i.e. improve consistency).

Imagery is useful in many situations and for many purposes. Some examples are given below and also in the Best Practice features. After reading the list, you might be able to make other suggestions:

- Goal-setting.
- Re-focusing.
- Positive thinking.
- Strategy development.
- Game preparation.
- Improving game focus/concentration.
- Self-belief and confidence.
- Increasing levels of motivation.
- Distraction training.
- Reducing anxiety in matches.

How to use imagery

Virtually everyone seems to have the ability to generate and use images, but not to the same degree. For some performers, imagery will be relatively unstructured without appearing to serve any specific purpose; they 'just do it' and may not be able to verbalize the exact content of their imagery. For others, the use of imagery will be very structured and will be practised to satisfy a variety of needs such as building self-confidence, enabling relaxation, learning new skills and focusing attention.

Imagery is more than simply seeing a picture (visualizing). To be most effective, players should be encouraged to use all their senses when imaging. They should see things in bright vivid colours, hear sounds, feel emotion and sense their surroundings. Emotions come into all good imagery, like feeling happy. The use of all the senses is referred to as 'kinaesthetic' imagery.

The analogy of a wide, flat-screen television could be used to illustrate imagery. Imagine a big screen with fantastic colours; you can see every detail in the image down to patterns on shirts, logos and shoelaces. You hear your teammates encouraging you, the spectators calling, the referee shouting instructions. The great thing about this TV is that you can feel the breeze against your face, can turn down the noises you don't need to hear (spectators), you can cut out the images that are not important and turn up the things you want!

Imagery ability refers to the vividness and controllability of the imagery. The ability to run imagery in slow motion or real time can be developed over time with practice, and players should be encouraged to try the different types of imagery.

The four R's

A good model to base imagery use on is the four R's model (Hale, 1998):

- Relaxation.
- Realism.
- Regularity.
- Reinforcement.

Imagery works best when a player is relaxed. Realism refers to making the image as real as possible – clear and vivid, and using all senses and feelings. To become really effective, as with any other skill, structured imagery should be used regularly (for example, for five minutes every day). Reinforcement can be achieved with the use of videos so that the player can really see themselves in action.

The ability to image a positive outcome is a crucial principle. If you think positively, you are more likely to succeed; if you think negatively, you are more likely to fail. Players who visualize themselves missing the target or making a mistake in execution are more likely to do so in matches.

Make your images as 'real' as possible

You need to experience every sense associated with every single aspect of the element of your performance that you intend to image. Can you feel the ball at your feet, its texture, its weight? Feel the strength in your legs and arms as you kick the ball (in your mind!). Feel the adrenaline and satisfaction that you experience as the ball leaves your foot. You should be able to see the pitch and be aware of the players around you and of your surroundings. Image the smell of the pitch, the smell of the ball, your own smell. Image the taste in your mouth, the sound of the crowd, the whistle, and the murmur of others around you.

- **You will need to practise incorporating the sensations of sound, smell, taste, sight, touch and, most important of all, feeling into your imagery training.**

- **Your imagery training should focus on quality not quantity.**

- **Imagery efforts can also be enhanced through watching videos of yourself performing. Watching an ideal or near ideal performance of yourself will help to create an effective image to use during your imagery practice.**

Imagery is an extremely versatile and valuable skill for which there are numerous uses:

- **For tactical rehearsal and problem solving** – imaging set-plays prior to a match will help you to store these tactics in your memory and further aid you in becoming clear and familiar with your roles.

- **To improve self-confidence** – by imaging previous, successful performances on a regular basis you will face competition in a more positive and confident frame of mind. During an unsuccessful performance, imaging previous successful performances will give you the motivation and confidence to repeat the same feat.

- **To feel and practise moves perfectly** – by recreating and 'feeling' an accurate technique in your mind, you will strengthen the blueprint for successful execution of the task in the future.

- **To correct or practice skills** – after physically working to correct a skill, imaging the correct skills will reinforce that information. Combining physical and mental practice is the most effective way of refining a skill.

- As preparation for performance – it is useful to image yourself performing well throughout a variety of conditions, i.e. bad weather, tough opponents, bad luck and umpire decisions. You will then be prepared for the unexpected.

- During injury – imaging your shot, interception, tackling, dribbling, past successful performances and tactics when you are unable to physically practice will aid you in maintaining mental freshness.

- As part of a pre-shot routine – imaging yourself with an accurate technique, e.g. successfully shooting, will aid consistent shooting in pressure situations. This method is ideal before taking a penalty or free kick and can also be used to recreate situations such as one vs. one duels, holding off a defender before shooting.

- To control anxiety and emotion – imaging relaxing scenes prior to a competition will work to calm your nerves. Try imaging lying on the beach in the sun to lower your emotional levels and perhaps image your national flag and the sound of your national anthem to psych yourself up; depending on whether you feel you need to lower or raise your emotional temperature.

- For performance review and analysis – imaging can aid your performance review if you use it to see both strong and weak points.

■   Ask your players to use imagery at night before going to sleep. At this time they should be quite relaxed. This imagery session could last for 10–15 minutes.

Ask each player to think about playing in their normal position and doing things they enjoy doing. A winger, for example, may constantly imagine themselves dribbling past defenders. This image could be continually rerun. Ask each player to try and use both internal and external perspectives and even change between each perspective. The players should use all of their senses. Ideally the image should have a start and finish so, for example, the players can be encouraged to see who passes the ball to them, and end with a cross or shot with a successful outcome.

Where and when to use imagery training

- At training sessions/home: Prior to performing a skill or combination of skills, the player should make the time to image each action as precisely and accurately as possible. They should move through the actions in their mind; experience themselves executing the skill perfectly; become actively involved in the imagery experience. Players can use a football as a prop for when they are imaging performing or practising a specific skill.

- At competitions: Before the game starts, the player should mentally recall their tactics, skills, movements or feelings that they would like to carry out.

Imagery can be used during both training and competition (particularly pre-match). Because of its ease of use, players can use imagery virtually anytime. Generally, players will use imagery more in conjunction with competition than with training, and it is not surprising that imagery is more prevalent prior to competing than at any other time. Imagery use before a match can help players feel more self-confident and in control of their emotion and stress levels. With respect to practice, players tend to use imagery more during practice than before or after practice. Outside of competition and practice, players use imagery during breaks in their daily activities (for instance, at work, school or home), and many routinely use imagery at night before going to sleep.

Imagery training is most effective when used with physical practice but, interestingly, imagery training is better than no practice at all. For an injured player or one unable to train, imagery training is ideal.

Best Practice Players can use imagery in the following situations: before going to sleep at night; pre-training or pre-match (two to three minutes); during training when practising repetitive drills or during breaks in matches (lasting for a matter of seconds); if they are substitutes – whilst on the line/bench.

Give it a go!

Now it is your turn to try imaging! Don't expect instant results. In fact, initially you may experience a decline in performance. You will need to systematically and regularly practise this mental skill as you would any physical skill. It is a good idea to make a place for imaging in your weekly training schedule. To begin with, focus on completing short sessions on a regular basis. Imaging two to three times a week for about five to ten minutes would be a good start. If you find your concentration breaking down and your attention faltering, take a break. Finally, persevere, it will take you a while before you become comfortable with this technique.

Team building is concerned with creating the right environment for players to develop 'free of fear'.

Setting realistic, specific and challenging team goals has a positive effect on the individual and team performance.

Imagery plays a crucial role in many players' preparation before a match or crucial passage of play. Players often speak about seeing success before it happens.

Parents are prime sources in the development of goals, values, beliefs and perceptions of their children.

Be a positive coach and recognize when players do well.

Confident players tend to play to win in that they want the ball, are not afraid to take chances and take control of the match.

Summary

- Imagery is a portable mental skill that can be used anywhere.

- Imagery can be used for motivational purposes.

- Imagery can be used for skill-learning purposes.

- Imagery can help enhance confidence.

- Try using imagery before going to sleep at night.

- Imagery is most effective when used together with actual physical training.

- Be as real as possible when using imagery and use all your senses.

- Use the wide-screen TV analogy and turn the colour up bright, the sound loud and be selective. You are the film director!

Self testers

1 What is imagery?
2 What two imagery perspectives can a player use?
3 Give three reasons for using imagery.
4 Suggest three times when imagery can be used.
5 What is meant by kinaesthetic imagery?

Action plan

Use your imagination   Develop a pre-match imagery script
with each of your players. Make the script personal to each player.
About five minutes before going out for your games, ask all players
to sit down and think about the game in their mind's eye. Ask them
to be as real as possible, using colours, sounds and feelings to see
themselves doing really well.

Chapter 9

Parent power

THIS CHAPTER WILL:

- Help you understand how influential parents are to player development.
- Explain how parents can positively effect player development.
- Describe the parent–coach–player relationship.
- Explore the different types of pre- and post-match effective talk.
- Explain the importance of emphasizing effort over result.
- Introduce the concept and importance of 'personal best'.

One of the most influential sources of a child's psychological and sociological development is his or her parents. A coach may interact with a young player from between one to five hours a week, but this pales into insignificance when compared with the time a parent spends with their child. It is primarily in the home that a child's beliefs, values, perceptions, attitudes and goals are shaped. Research has shown that the interest and support of parents is vital to a young player's continued participation in sport. It has, however, also shown that much of the pressure and anxiety that young players feel in sport can come from their parents. Parents have an extremely influential role to play in their child's football experience, whatever the level of their involvement, but this can be of a positive and constructive or negative and destructive nature.

So why do parents become so animated and involved in their child's sport? Parents often have a strong desire to make things right; this 'righting reflex' has a tendency to make parents overzealous in their attitude towards their child. This well-intentioned desire can lead to confrontation instead of collaboration; telling the child what he or she should or should not have done rather than respecting the child and believing that the child has the answer, and encouraging them. Some parents may perceive that their child's competence is their competence. They may wish to live or relive their sporting experience through their child and assume that their child has to do as they did. A child's participation in football can offer parents the opportunity to rewind their own sport experience and make up for their perceived failures and missed opportunities.

What's the purpose of it all?

The best starting point for becoming a good football parent is to give careful consideration to the purpose of your child playing football. This reflection fundamentally concerns the 'why' of football. Questions which are useful to ask your child, and perhaps more importantly to ask yourself first, are, 'Why is your child playing football?' or, 'Why do you want them to play football?', 'Why invest all the time, money, sacrifice, and hard work?', 'What's the purpose of it all?', 'What does success for your child, in football, look like to you?', 'How is success of your child's involvement in football defined and measured by you and your child?'

One of the all-time great Australian coaches, a man named Percy Cerutty, who was an athletics coach and coach to Herb Elliott, the Olympic gold medallist of the 1,500 m at the 1960 Rome Olympics, once said to Herb Elliott:

Quote | 'The only justification for you devoting part of your life to this sport, is that you're going to grow into a better human being.'
Herb Elliott, *Winning Attitudes*, 2000

Dan Gould, an eminent North American sport psychologist conducted some research on the development of US Olympic champions. He stated:

Quote | 'The importance of not pressurising athletes to "win early" in their careers, but to teach values such as hard work, optimism and a "can do" attitude seem paramount . . . At the same time, parents emphasised the attitude, *"if you are going to do it, do it right"*. They also modelled a hard work ethic, held high (but reasonable) expectations and standards for their child, and emphasised a stick to it and follow through on commitments attitude.'
Dan Gould, *The Development of Psychological Talent in US Olympic Champions*, 2002

Quote | 'Excellence is all about attitude.
Attitude is all about environment.
Parents influence the environment.'

Good football parenting – it's not easy!

It is not easy to be a good parent, and it is even harder to be a good parent of a competitive football player. To know what is best to do and say, and when to say and do it, can be difficult. It can be more daunting for parents who have not been involved in the football scene. There are many questions to ask and often quite a few people who are only too prepared to offer you their answers! Many problems arise because parents are unsure of the best way to help their child and so use their natural instincts, which can often lead to ineffective and sometimes destructive solutions. For example, to try and increase the confidence of their child prior to a match before going on the pitch to warm up, a parent might say, 'Go on Helen, just do your best. You know you're better than their central mid-fielder, so just go and show it!' On the face of it, this sounds encouraging, but if you're Helen, you may feel some pressure – you are now aware that a comparison will be made by your parents between you and the opposition's central mid-fielder.

Coach–parent working alliance – showing empathy

As a coach it may be best to involve parents and work with them, rather than exclude them. The perception and spirit of this interaction is perhaps most appropriately encompassed in comparing the following two titles of workshops. One was called, 'Dealing with parents', and the other, 'Working with parents'. Implicit in the wording of the first title is a certain defensive, almost confrontational, tone and approach; whereas the second suggests more of a collaborative stand.

Being a football parent can be hard work. If coaches can show empathy for parents, the working alliance between coaches and parents will be enhanced. Empathy is about being able to communicate with another person from their internal viewpoint – to see things with their eyes. An example of empathy and a collaborative, rather than confrontational, style can be seen in the following dialogue:

Ineffective communication

Coach: How did Chris do in his trial?

Parent: Oh! I don't know why I bother . . . he seemed flat and didn't seem to care. He was slow to the ball and didn't really get stuck in.

Then . . .

Coach: Have you thought of getting him to do some short sprints just before he goes on, to energize him?

Parent: I could do I suppose, but he just doesn't seem to want it! I sometimes wonder whether it's worth all this time and effort.

Coach: It sounds as though he's nervous . . . the sprints will help him to get rid of nerves.

Parent: Well, I don't know, but something has to change.

Effective communication

Coach: How did Chris do in his trial?

Parent: Oh! I don't know why I bother . . . he seemed flat and didn't seem to care. He was slow to the ball and didn't really get stuck in.

Then . . .

Coach: It sounds frustrating. (Coach showing empathy)

Parent: Yes, it is . . . . I know he doesn't mean it, but it's just that we're putting a lot of time in.

Coach: It can't be easy, when you're not sure what your son wants from football.

Dangerous assumptions

In order to communicate effectively with parents, a coach needs to enter into the relationship with an open and unbiased mind. The parents have to do likewise. It is important that the coach is aware of possible 'perception traps' that, if avoided, will lead to improved rapport with parents. Dangerous assumptions that the coach should be aware of include:

- **The parents are going to be difficult.**
- **The parents are in it for the wrong reasons – they just want their son or daughter to be a professional footballer.**
- **The parents are only here as taxi drivers.**
- **The parents do not know anything about the sport.**
- **The parents think they know everything about the sport.**
- **I am the expert – they must follow my advice.**

What can parents do to create an appropriate environment for their child so that their child will have the best chance of developing a healthy attitude towards competition and football?

The 'word on your street'

The words you use in your language while involved in youth football will significantly impact on your player's motivational style towards football. Having the word 'effort' as the cornerstone of your 'football language' will go a long way to develop a person who has an assured and healthy approach towards life and football. Be careful of using the word 'should', for example, 'They should have won', 'You should have scored'. Words like 'should' and 'ought' are verbs of obligation. Players may feel obliged to do things when your sentences are preceded by 'should'.

Consistent feedback

What questions do parents ask when their child comes home after playing a match, is it 'Did you win?', 'What was the score?', or 'How did you play?'

After asking the more performance-oriented question of, 'How did you play?' be careful that you receive a performance-oriented answer rather

than the often-heard response of, 'Oh, we lost 3–2' or, 'We won 5–1'. You then have to be careful not to be satisfied with the, 'We won 5–1' response more than the 'Oh, we lost 3–2' version. To allow the player to fully understand that performance is key and that, 'the match isn't over until the lesson has been learned', the same amount of feedback needs to be elicited whether the player (the team) has won or lost, played well or poorly. Far too often there is more feedback asked for and offered by parents after a victory than after a loss.

Avoid using the word 'we' such as, 'We have a game on Friday' or 'We played well today'. After all it is their match, their practice, their football.

Decrease the 'but'; increase the 'and'

As mentioned in Chapter 3, try to decrease your use of the word 'but' and increase your use of the word 'and'. For example, 'You played well

Fiona, but if you can get in more crosses earlier that would help' to be replaced with, 'You played well Fiona, and if you can get in more crosses earlier that would help'. It is often said by using the word 'but' that the words before it have then been reduced in importance. In the example given, the 'but' detracts from the positive part of the feedback. The 'played well' is not heard. All the young footballer hears is the instructional part of the feedback and because it was preceded by a 'but', the player's confidence is momentarily lowered and she then perceives the neutral statement of 'if you can get in more crosses earlier that would help' as negative and slightly critical. Using the word 'and' maintains the positive feelings of competence from the first part of the feedback, while giving more self-confidence to the player by providing them with hope and the perception that they can get even better. In summary, 'buts' tend to take away, whereas 'ands' add on.

Feedback on effort

Beliefs about the causes of success are fundamental to the understanding of achievement-motivated behaviour in sport. Ego orientation is closely related with beliefs that 'ability' is to be honoured and valued, whereas it is effort that is prized within task orientation. If parents are able to help players believe that success in sport is due to persistence and effort which is controllable, rather than ability which is often perceived as uncontrollable, then players will see that there is always hope. Hope brings confidence and an ability to bounce back after set-backs. Effort is also a quality which is transferable into other areas of a player's life rather than merely a skill confined to the football pitch. Moreover, effort is an attribute fundamental to improving as a footballer. One of the best opportunities a parent has of instilling the concept that effort is to be truly honoured and valued is by providing some critical feedback to the player and/or team after success has been achieved, but through low effort. Taking this 'golden opportunity' will help the player(s) to recognize that the process is more valued than the outcome.

Pre- and post-match talks

Logically and simply, pre- and post-match talks are about the verbal expectations of the parents before the match and the 'emotional state' they create within their child. They are also concerned with what parents emphasize and the way they feed back information after the match.

Before playing a match, what would a player like to feel or how would they like to be? Feelings such as confident, positive and challenged are often associated with effective and enjoyable performances in sport. A pre-match talk in which emphasis is placed upon what the player can control is significant in increasing confidence. A player does not necessarily have to have confidence in their ability to win the match. However, they do need confidence in their ability to achieve something with their control. Behaviours such as effort, SMART performance and process goals should be focused upon.

Before performing, players need to direct their thinking to the process or *'the how'* of what they need to do rather than to the outcome in order to control their anxiety or nervous tension, to enhance their self-confidence and to ensure that they have the appropriate level of arousal or 'emotional temperature'. It is therefore helpful if, through pre-match talks, parents can provide PACE to their child before they face the opposition:

PACE before you face

- **Process.**
- **Anxiety.**
- **Confidence.**
- **Emotional temperature.**

What could parents and coaches say to a player before they go on the pitch to provide some PACE to the player before they compete?

- 'Challenge yourself and learn.'
- 'Enjoy the challenges you give yourself and learn.'
- Work hard to achieve your goals, and have fun.'
- 'If you can give 100 per cent, you can never lose.'
- 'Do you think you can finish the match a better player?'
- 'On a scale of one to ten how confident are you that you can finish the match a better player?'

Another way to help the player go into the match feeling confident, optimally aroused, with the right level of nervous tension and with a competitive yet 'personal-best' attitude is to ask the player a question to elicit feelings of this 'emotional mix'. Encourage them to talk and so verbally persuade themselves about how confident, positive and challenged they are. Questions such as:

- 'How do you want to be on the pitch today?'
- 'What personal strengths and skills do you have that give you some confidence that you will play well today?'
- 'When are you a really good football player?'
- 'What do you think you can guarantee on the pitch today?'
- 'What other good things do you think you will find out about yourself today?'
- 'What do you think you will want to do to finish the match a better player?'

If you really want to win, the most effective way to do this is not to focus on winning! Winning and very good performances need to be broken down into 'winning behaviours'. These are the building blocks of winning, and these, whatever they may be for the player and team, should be emphasized and evaluated.

Performance reviews need to be consistent no matter whether the performance is good or bad, or the outcome is a win or a loss. If your child does not try hard or does not play well, it is important to depersonalize your feedback, so that it is based on skills and behaviour rather than on personality. For example, 'I do not like it when you give up' rather than, 'I don't like you when you give up'. Feedback should be provided about deficiencies in performance, not deficiencies in the person. You will know when you have got it right in post-match discussions when you are doing more listening than talking. By listening carefully and gently directing the conversation, you will encourage your child to reflect more on what has happened. If the player appears to be working harder than the parent (or coach), and often realizing things about their performance for the first time, you are on the track to developing a self-determining person.

Best Practice Be consistent with your feedback quantity and quality, no matter what the outcome or the performance.

'Me then, me now' comparisons

One of the most significant actions you can take as a coach or parent is to change football into a personal-best sport, so giving your player more of a PB mentality. Sports in which performance can be easily and accurately measured and recorded such as athletics, gymnastics, swimming and golf allow participants to experience considerable success and feelings of confidence even though they may not win. Putting systems into place that enable your player to strive to improve their PB performance will encourage them to have a greater sense of control over what happens, and will provide far greater opportunities for building self-confidence. One of the most productive ways to do this is to work with your player to set some short-term SMART goals (see Chapter 7).

Explaining success and failure

How people explain success and failure can have a significant bearing on their self-confidence and their feelings of what they can and cannot control within football. It is mentally healthy if you can take responsibility for your actions, rather than making excuses for yourself. When a player

or team is successful, it is helpful to explain this success with reference to the players' or team's ability rather than luck or the opponent's poor play. After experiencing a failure, it can be healthy to explain the failure through lack of effort or inappropriate tactics, both of which are controllable and can be changed. If the reason for the failure is given as lack of ability, it must be stressed that this is current lack of ability. The players' perception of their ability is something that can be controlled and thus improved by themselves.

■ Consider your thoughts and feelings in the following scenarios, and your consequent post-match talk and behaviour:

1 Player plays poorly and team win.
2 Player plays well and team win.
3 Player plays poorly and team lose.
4 Player plays well and team lose.

The main objectives after success or failure are to:

- **Enhance self-confidence at every possible opportunity.**
- **Increase motivation.**
- **Increase awareness.**
- **Nurture responsibility – for what happened and then consequently your child will feel that they can then do something about it.**

Quote | 'You might lose the match, but don't lose the lesson!'

Making the journey

In order to help your child's journey through football to be a satisfying and long-lasting one, encourage them to travel by CAR!

> **Competence**
> **Autonomy**
> **Relatedness**

Competence

At every possible opportunity, find ways to make your child feel as though they are competent, not only at football but in other activities as well, as this will improve their overall confidence (self-esteem) as well as specific confidence in aspects of their football.

Autonomy

People have a basic human need to be in control of their lives and what happens to them. People are motivated to be what is called 'self-determined' – *'I do it because I want to!'*. It is therefore important that parents encourage their children to be responsible and independent. Avoid making them overly dependent on you. Nurture freedom of choice within your child by asking for their opinion and being prepared to listen.

Relatedness

People need to relate to, care for and be related to and cared for by others. Developing relationships with others is an important motive for people.

Summary

Parents are prime sources in the development of goals, values, beliefs, and perceptions of their children. They play a critical role in their child's motivational development. Their role not only involves the quality of their visual and verbal behaviours but also how proactive they are in reinforcing and 'coming alongside' the coach, assuming the coach displays the appropriate motivational behaviour themselves. If parents can nurture their child's responsibility, increase their awareness and enhance their self-confidence, then their 'parent power' will allow them to **empower** their child!

- **Parents or guardians may well be the most influential people in the young player's development.**
- **Develop the parent–coach–player relationship.**
- **Be aware of how your words can effect your son/daughter's development and performance.**

Self testers

1 What is the 'word on your street'?
2 What should you offer the most feedback on?
3 Give three different pre-match statements that may help performance.
4 How would you best explain 'success' and 'failure'.

Action plan

Assess achievement   Develop a means of assessing your son/daughter's personal-best achievements in matches. Use easily measurable actions such as accurate passes with left or right foot, shoots on target, ability to switch play etc. Do not simply record wins or losses.

Conclusion

THIS CHAPTER WILL:
- Summarize the main concepts discussed in this book.
- Offer advice on 'What next?'.

A key reason for studying sport psychology in football is to improve your awareness of players as individuals – why they play, what motivates them, how to improve their confidence, control and commitment and, most of all, how to ensure players continue to have fun during their development.

Creating a positive football environment can help to bring your sessions to life. When you spend time developing as a coach, but you feel that your players are not progressing at the rate they should be, it may be that on a psychological level something needs your attention. Armed with some of the basic information in this book, you can now start looking at issues such as motivation, confidence, goal-setting and communication in a more informed and critical way. By carrying out the Tasks and Action plans in the book, and adapting them to suit your own style and your own players, you will be on your way to becoming an even better coach.

Quote | 'The quality of a person's life is in direct proportion to their commitment to excellence.'

The most important message to take away from this book is that you may be the most influential person in your players' football development. Your actions and your feedback may ultimately decide whether your players ever reach their true potential. By creating a positive, safe environment, where players are free to develop without the fear of making mistakes, or as Sven Göran Eriksson would say, without the 'fear of failure', you will ensure that players blossom into the best players they can become, and that they will also develop as people. For you, the coach, this can be a great challenge and a rewarding privilege. Treat it with the respect it deserves!

LEARNING

Summary

Sport psychology plays a massive part in sport today. In the future, more players will use the benefits of sport-psychology techniques. As players are offered more and more choices in sports, activities, computer and video games, it is essential that their football experience continues to be one in which they can have fun, experience pleasure while training and playing competitive matches, and continue to develop and improve their skills in a safe and positive environment.

Self testers

1   What is the main thing you have learned from this book?

2   Will you continue to implement some of the suggestions in both your training sessions and in competitive situations?

3   Will you be a player-centred coach?

Action plan

Keep learning   Check out the FA Sport Psychology online courses to develop your knowledge of the basic principles of sport psychology at **www.TheFA.com**.

Try to read some of the material referenced at the back of this book, and enjoy the benefits!

LEARNING

References and recommended readings

Beswick, B. (2001). *Focused on Soccer*. Human Kinetics.

Crisfield, P., Cabral, P. and Carpenter, F. *The Successful Coach*. National Coaching Foundation.

Elliot, H. (2000). *Winning Attitudes*. Hardie Grant Books in association with Australian Olympic Committee.

Eriksson, S. (2001). *Sven-Göran Eriksson on Football*. Carlton Books.

Forzoni, R. (2001). 'Motivation in Football – part 1'. *Insight Magazine*. Issue 3, vol 4, 56–8.

Forzoni, R. (2001). 'Motivation in Football – part 2'. *Insight Magazine*. Issue 4, vol 4, 31–3.

Forzoni, R. 'Sport Psychology in Football . . . does it really work?' *Insight Magazine*, Issue 4, vol 6, 62–4.

Gould, Daniel, PhD., Kristen Dieffenbach, M. S. and Aaron Moffett, M. S. (2001). *The Development of Psychological Talent in U.S. Olympic Champions*.

Hale, B. (1998). *Imagery Training*. National Coaching Foundation.

Lowther, J., Lane, A. M., and Lane, H. J. (2002). *Self-efficacy and psychological skills during the amputee soccer world cup.*

Lowther, J., Carlow, A., and Lovell, G. *A comparison of motivational orientations in professional, semi professional and amateur soccer players,* BASES and BASEM Conference, 3rd–6th September 2003. Sheffield Hallam University.

Martens, R. (1987). *Coaches Guide to Sport Psychology.* Human Kinetics.

Orlick, T. and Partington, J. (1988). 'Mental Links to Excellence'. *The Sport Psychologist,* 2, 105–130.

Riley, P. (1994). *The Winner Within. A Life Plan for Team Players.* Berkley Business.

Rotella, B. (1995). *Golf is not a game of perfect.* Simon and Schuster.

Walton, G. M. (1992). *Beyond Winning.* Human Kinetics.

Weingburg, R. S. & Gould, D. (2003). *Foundations of Sport & Exercise Psychology.* Human Kinetics.

Wein, H. (2001). *Developing Youth soccer Players.* Wein Human Kinetics.

The Successful Coach-guidelines for coaching practice. Sports Coach UK, 2003.

LEARNING

Contacts

Fédération Internationale de Football Association (FIFA)
FIFA House
Hitzigweg 11
PO Box 85
8030 Zurich
Switzerland
Tel: +41-43/222 7777
Fax: +41-43/222 7878
Internet: http://www.fifa.com

Confederations

Asian Football Confederation (AFC)
AFC House, Jalan 1/155B
Bukit Jalil
Kuala Lumpur 57000
Malaysia
Tel: +60-3/8994 3388
Fax: +60-3/8994 2689
Internet: http://www.footballasia.com

Confédération Africaine de Football (CAF)
3 Abdel Khalek Sarwat Street
El Hay El Motamayez
PO Box 23
6th October City
Egypt
Tel: +20-2/837 1000
Fax: +20-2/837 0006
Internet: http://www.cafonline.com

Confederation of North, Central American and Caribbean Association Football (CONCACAF)
Central American and Caribbean Association Football
725 Fifth Avenue, 17th Floor
New York, NY 10022
USA
Tel: +1-212/308 0044
Fax: +1-212/308 1851
Internet: http://www.concacaf.net

Confederación Sudamericana de Fútbol (CONMEBOL)
Autopista Aeropuerto Internacional y
Leonismo Luqueño
Luque (Gran Asunción)
Paraguay
Tel: +595-21/645 781
Fax: +595-21/645 791
Internet: http://www.conmebol.com

Oceania Football Confederation (OFC)
Ericsson Stadium
12 Maurice Road
PO Box 62 586
Penrose
Auckland
New Zealand
Tel: +64-9/525 8161
Fax: +64-9/525 8164
Internet: http://www.oceaniafootball
.com

Union European Football Association (UEFA)
Route de Genève 46
Nyon 1260
Switzerland
Tel: +41-22/994 4444
Fax: +41-22/994 4488
Internet: http://www.uefa.com

Associations
Argentina
Asociación del Fútbol Argentino (AFA)
Viamonte 1366/76
Buenos Aires 1053
Tel: ++54-11/4372 7900
Fax: ++54-11/4375 4410
Internet: http://www.afa.org.ar

Australia
Soccer Australia Limited (ASF)
Level 3
East Stand, Stadium Australia
Edwin Flack Avenue
Homebush NSW 2127
Tel: ++61-2/9739 5555
Fax: ++61-2/9739 5590
Internet: http://www.socceraustralia
.com.au

Belgium
Union Royale Belge des Sociétés de Football Assocation (URBSFA/KBV)
145 Avenue Houba de Strooper
Bruxelles 1020
Tel: ++32-2/477 1211
Fax: ++32-2/478 2391
Internet: http://www.footbel.com

Brazil
Confederação Brasileira de Futebol (CBF)
Rua Victor Civita 66
Bloco 1 – Edifício 5 – 5 Andar
Barra da Tijuca
Rio de Janeiro 22775-040
Tel: ++55-21/3870 3610
Fax: ++55-21/3870 3612
Internet: http://www.cbfnews.com

Cameroon
Fédération Camerounaise de Football (FECAFOOT)
Case postale 1116
Yaoundé
Tel: ++237/221 0012
Fax: ++237/221 6662
Internet: http://www.cameroon.fifa.com

Canada
**The Canadian Soccer Association
(CSA)**
Place Soccer Canada
237 Metcalfe Street
Ottawa ONT K2P 1R2
Tel: ++1-613/237 7678
Fax: ++1-613/237 1516
Internet: http://www.canadasoccer.com

Costa Rica
**Federación Costarricense de
Fútbol (FEDEFUTBOL)**
Costado Norte Estatua León Cortés
San José 670-1000
Tel: ++506/222 1544
Fax: ++506/255 2674
Internet: http://www.fedefutbol.com

Croatia
Croatian Football Federation (HNS)
Rusanova 13
Zagreb 10 000
Tel: ++385-1/236 1555
Fax: ++385-1/244 1501
Internet: http://www.hns-cff.hr

Czech Republic
**Football Association of Czech
Republic (CMFS)**
Diskarska 100
Praha 6 16017
Tel: ++420-2/3302 9111
Fax: ++420-2/3335 3107
Internet: http://www.fotbal.cz

Denmark
**Danish Football Association
(DBU)**
Idrættens Hus
Brøndby Stadion 20
Brøndby 2605
Tel: ++45-43/262 222
Fax: ++45-43/262 245
Internet: http://www.dbu.dk

England
The Football Association (The FA)
25 Soho Square
London W1D 4FA
Tel: ++44-207/745 4545
Fax: ++44-207/745 4546
Internet: http://www.TheFA.com

Finland
Suomen Palloliitto (SPL/FBF)
Urheilukatu 5
PO Box 191
Helsinki 00251
Tel: ++358-9/7421 51
Fax: ++358-9/7421 5200
Internet: http://www.palloliitto.fi

France
**Fédération Française de Football
(FFF)**
60 Bis Avenue d'Iéna
Paris 75116
Tel: ++33-1/4431 7300
Fax: ++33-1/4720 8296
Internet: http://www.fff.fr

Germany
Deutscher Fussball-Bund (DFB)
Otto-Fleck-Schneise 6
Postfach 71 02 65
Frankfurt Am Main 60492
Tel: ++49-69/678 80
Fax: ++49-69/678 8266
Internet: http://www.dfb.de

Greece
Hellenic Football Federation (HFF)
137 Singrou Avenue
Nea Smirni
Athens 17121
Tel: ++30-210/930 6000
Fax: ++30-210/935 9666
Internet: http://www.epo.gr

Ireland Republic
The Football Association of Ireland (FAI)
80 Merrion Square, South
Dublin 2
Tel: ++353-1/676 6864
Fax: ++353-1/661 0931
Internet: http://www.fai.ie

Italy
Federazione Italiana Giuoco Calcio (FIGC)
Via Gregorio Allegri, 14
Roma 00198
Tel: ++39-06/84 911
Fax: ++39-06/84 912 526
Internet: http://www.figc.it

Japan
Japan Football Association (JFA)
JFA House
3-10-15, Hongo
Bunkyo-ku
Tokyo 113-0033
Tel: ++81-3/3830 2004
Fax: ++81-3/3830 2005
Internet: http://www.jfa.or.jp

Kenya
Kenya Football Federation (KFF)
PO Box 40234
Nairobi
Tel: ++254-2/608 422
Fax: ++254-2/249 855
Email: kff@todays.co.ke

Korea Republic
Korea Football Association (KFA)
1-131 Sinmunno, 2-ga
Jongno-Gu
Seoul 110-062
Tel: ++82-2/733 6764
Fax: ++82-2/735 2755
Internet: http://www.kfa.or.kr

Mexico
Federación Mexicana de Fútbol Asociación, A.C. (FMF)
Colima No. 373
Colonia Roma
Mexico, D.F. 06700
Tel: ++52-55/5241 0190
Fax: ++52-55/5241 0191
Internet: http://www.femexfut.org.mx

Netherlands
Koninklijke Nederlandse Voetbalbond (KNVB)
Woudenbergseweg 56–58
PO Box 515
Am Zeist 3700 AM
Tel: ++31-343/499 201
Fax: ++31-343/499 189
Internet: http://www.knvb.nl

Nigeria
Nigeria Football Association (NFA)
Plot 2033, Olusegun
Obasanjo Way, Zone 7, Wuse Abuja
PO Box 5101 Garki
Abuja
Tel: ++234-9/523 7326
Fax: ++234-9/523 7327
Email: nfa@microaccess.com

Northern Ireland
Irish Football Association Ltd. (IFA)
20 Windsor Avenue
Belfast BT9 6EE
Tel: ++44-28/9066 9458
Fax: ++44-28/9066 7620
Internet: http://www.irishfa.com

Paraguay
Asociación Paraguaya de Fútbol (APF)
Estadio de los Defensores del Chaco
Calle Mayor Martinez 1393
Asunción
Tel: ++595-21/480 120
Fax: ++595-21/480 124
Internet: http://www.apf.org.py

Poland
Polish Football Association (PZPN)
Polski Zwiazek Pilki Noznej
Miodowa 1
Warsaw 00-080
Tel: ++48-22/827 0914
Fax: ++48-22/827 0704
Internet: http://www.pzpn.pl

Portugal
Federação Portuguesa de Futebol (FPF)
Praça de Alegria, N. 25
PO Box 21.100
Lisbon 1250-004
Tel: ++351-21/325 2700
Fax: ++351-21/325 2780
Internet: http://www.fpf.pt

Romania
Romanian Football Federation (FRF)
House of Football
Str. Serg. Serbanica Vasile 12
Bucharest 73412
Tel: ++40-21/325 0678
Fax: ++40-21/325 0679
Internet: http://www.frf.ro

Russia
Football Union of Russia (RFU)
8 Luzhnetskaya Naberezhnaja
Moscow 119 992
Tel: ++7-095/201 1637
Fax: ++7-502/220 2037
Internet: http://www.rfs.ru

Scotland
The Scottish Football Association (SFA)
Hampden Park
Glasgow G42 9AY
Tel: ++44-141/616 6000
Fax: ++44-141/616 6001
Internet: http://www.scottishfa.co.uk

South Africa
South African Football Association (SAFA)
First National Bank Stadium
PO Box 910
Johannesburg 2000
Tel: ++27-11/494 3522
Fax: ++27-11/494 3013
Internet: http://www.safa.net

Spain
Real Federación Española de Fútbol (RFEF)
Ramon y Cajal, s/n
Apartado postale 385
Madrid 28230
Tel: ++34-91/495 9800
Fax: ++34-91/495 9801
Internet: http://www.rfef.es

Sweden
Svenska Fotbollförbundet (SVFF)
PO Box 1216
Solna 17 123
Tel: ++46-8/735 0900
Fax: ++46-8/735 0901
Internet: http://www.svenskfotboll.se

Switzerland
Schweizerischer Fussball-Verband (SFV/ASF)
Postfach
Bern 15 3000
Tel: ++41-31/950 8111
Fax: ++41-31/950 8181
Internet: http://www.football.ch

Tunisia
Fédération Tunisienne de Football (FTF)
Maison des Fédérations Sportives
Cité Olympique
Tunis 1003
Tel: ++216-71/233 303
Fax: ++216-71/767 929
Internet: http://www.ftf.org.tn

Turkey
Türkiye Futbol Federasyonu (TFF)
Konaklar Mah. Ihlamurlu Sok. 9
4. Levent
Istanbul 80620
Tel: ++90-212/282 7020
Fax: ++90-212/282 7015
Internet: http://www.tff.org

United States of America
US Soccer Federation (USSF)
US Soccer House
1801 S. Prairie Avenue
Chicago IL 60616
Tel: ++1-312/808 1300
Fax: ++1-312/808 1301
Internet: http://www.ussoccer.com

Uruguay
Asociación Uruguaya de Fútbol (AUF)
Guayabo 1531
Montevideo 11200
Tel: ++59-82/400 4814
Fax: ++59-82/409 0550
Internet: http://www.auf.org.uy

Wales
The Football Association of Wales, Ltd (FAW)
Plymouth Chambers
3 Westgate Street
Cardiff CF10 1DP
Tel: ++44-29/2037 2325
Fax: ++44-29/2034 3961
Internet: http://www.faw.org.uk

For details of County FAs please see **www.TheFA.com**/Grassroots

LEARNING

Index

All about FA Learning

FA Learning is the Educational Division of The FA and is responsible for the delivery, co-ordination and promotion of its extensive range of educational products and services. This includes all courses and resources for coaching, refereeing, psychology, sports science, medical exercise, child protection, crowd safety and teacher training.

The diverse interests of those involved in football ensures that FA Learning remains committed to providing resources and activities suitable for all individuals whatever their interests, experience or level of expertise.

Whether you're a Premier League Manager, sports psychologist or interested parent, our aim is to have courses and resources available that will improve your knowledge and understanding.

If you've enjoyed reading this book and found the content useful then why not take a look at FA Learning's website to find out the types of courses and additional resources available to help you continue your football development.

The website contains information on all the national courses and events managed by The FA as well as information on a number of online resources:

- **Psychology for Soccer Level 1 – Our first online qualification.**
- **Soccer Star – Free online coaching tool for young players.**
- **Soccer Parent – Free online course for parents.**

All these resources can be accessed at home from your own PC and are currently used by thousands of people across the world.

Psychology for Soccer Level 1

Enrol today and join hundreds of others around the world taking part in FA Learning's first ever online qualification.

This pioneering project is the first of its kind to be provided by any Football Governing Body and is available to anyone with access to the internet. There are no additional qualifications required to take part other than an interest in learning more about the needs of young players and an email address!

The course is aimed at coaches, parents and teachers of 7–12 year olds looking to gain an introduction to psychology and features modules based on 'true to life' player, coach and parent scenarios.

Psychology for Soccer Level 1 is a completely interactive, multimedia learning experience. Don't just take our word for it, read some of the comments from those that have already completed the course:

'Wow what a wonderful course! Thank you for the time and effort to make this possible.' **Tracy Scott**

'Just passed the final assessment ... it was a good experience to learn this way and hopefully more qualifications will become available in this format. Thanks.' **Shayne Hall**

'I am a professional football coach working in schools and clubs and have travelled all around the world. I have really enjoyed the literature in this course and it has made me think about how I should address my coaching sessions. I want to progress in the field of sport psychology and this course has whetted my appetite for this subject.' **Chris Rafael Sabater**

The course modules are:

- Psychology and Soccer
- Motivation
- Learning and Acquiring skills
- Psychological Development
- Environment and Social Influences

In addition to the five course modules, learners also have access to a number of further benefits included as part of the course fee. The benefits include:

- **Three months support from qualified FA tutors**
- **Classroom specific online discussion forums**
- **A global online discussion forum**
- **All successful students receive a FA Qualification in psychology**

- **An exclusive resource area containing over 100 articles and web links relating to coaching 7–12 year olds.**

Within the five modules, there are over 20 sessions totaling over eight hours worth of content. Including the use of discussion forums, resource area and the course tasks, we anticipate the course will take on average 20 hours to complete.

For more information and to enroll on the course visit www.**TheFA.com**/FALearning.

THE OFFICIAL FA GUIDE TO
BASIC TEAM COACHING

Be a part of the game

The Official FA Guide to Basic Team Coaching covers all the essential aspects of coaching and is vital for those who coach amateur football, or who are considering becoming a coach.

This book includes:
- **team strategies and tactics**
- **leadership and management**
- **match analysis.**

Packed with practical exercises, information and expert advice, this book will improve your understanding and enhance your ability and enjoyment of the world's greatest game.

The author, **Les Reed**, is The FA's Acting Technical Director and was formerly the Assistant Manager at Charlton Athletic. Les has coached England players at every level from youth to senior teams.

FA Learning
'learning through football'

TheFA.com/FALearning

Visit the website for information on all FA Learning's educational activities.

THE OFFICIAL FA GUIDE TO
FITNESS FOR FOOTBALL

Be a part of the game

The Official FA Guide to Fitness for Football provides essential knowledge and advice for everyone who plays the game.

This book includes:
- **basic physiology and nutrition**
- **training strategies**
- **the physiological differences between adults and children.**

Packed with practical exercises, information and expert advice, this book will improve your understanding and enhance your ability and enjoyment of the world's greatest game.

The author, **Dr Richard Hawkins**, is the Deputy Head of Exercise Science at The Football Association.

FA Learning
'learning through football'

TheFA.com/FALearning

Visit the website for information on all FA Learning's educational activities.

The FA

LEARNING

THE OFFICIAL FA GUIDE TO
RUNNING A TEAM

Be a part of the game

The Official FA Guide to Running a Team is written for anyone involved in the administration side of the game.

This book includes:
- **advice on how to start and run a team**
- **who to turn to for help**
- **how to deal with any problems that may occur**
- **finance, administration, PR and marketing.**

Packed with practical exercises, information and expert advice, this book will improve your understanding and enhance your ability and enjoyment of the world's greatest game.

The author, **Les Howie**, is responsible for the development of all clubs in the non-professional national game for The Football Association

FA Learning
'learning through football'

TheFA.com/FALearning

Visit the website for information on all FA Learning's educational activities.

THE OFFICIAL FA GUIDE TO
BASIC REFEREEING

Be a part of the game

The Official FA Guide to Basic Refereeing is essential reading for all referees and those in training, and also provides vital knowledge for anyone involved in the game.

This book includes:
- **the laws of the game and how to apply them**
- **recognising free kick and offside offences**
- **important advice about managing players.**

Packed with practical exercises, information and expert advice, this book will improve your understanding and enhance your ability and enjoyment of the world's greatest game.

The author, **John Baker**, is Head of Refereeing at The Football Association, responsible for the 30,000 registered referees in England.

FA Learning
'learning through football'

TheFA.com/FALearning

Visit the website for information on all FA Learning's educational activities.

THE OFFICIAL FA GUIDE:
A PARENT'S GUIDE TO FOOTBALL

Be a part of the game

The Official FA Guide: A Parent's Guide to Football is essential reading for any parent of a young footballer, who wants to get involved and help their child to do their very best.

This book includes:
- **choosing a club and being involved in it**
- **sharing the football interest**
- **being a 'garden coach'.**

Packed with practical exercises, information and expert advice, this book will improve your understanding and enhance your ability and enjoyment of the world's greatest game.

The author, **Les Howie,** is responsible for the development of all clubs in the non-professional national game for The Football Association.

FA Learning
'learning through football'

TheFA.com/FALearning

Visit the website for information on all FA Learning's educational activities.